"Stress Nation *by Justin Hai is a game-changer for anyone looking to reclaim their health in our tech-driven world. With a perfect blend of science and practical wisdom, Justin shines a light on how screens are sabotaging our hormones and well-being – and offers a clear path to restore balance. A must-read for anyone ready to thrive, not just survive!"*

*—**Jason Vieth**,*
CEO of Laird Superfood

"Stress Nation *is a timely, eye-opening exploration of how our screen obsessed culture is quietly eroding our health, happiness, and human connection. Justin Hai's book illuminates the effect of keeping up in a world that doesn't slow down and how to reclaim your balance and well-being in the relentless pace of modern life. It's the reset you didn't know you needed."*

*—**Wendy Collie**,*
Former Executive Starbucks Coffee,
Founder and CEO of Better Way Business

"Justin Hai's Stress Nation *is a must-read wake-up call – insightful, practical, and deeply needed in our screen-obsessed world. A powerful guide to reclaiming balance."*

*—**Fabian Seelbach**,*
Former Executive of Curology, goop, and CEO of Cometeer

"Stress Nation *is a compelling wake-up call for anyone feeling drained by the digital age. With a perfect blend of science, and storytelling, Justin Hai unpacks the hidden hormonal havoc caused by our screen-obsessed culture – and more importantly, shows us how to reclaim our health, our sleep, and our sanity. A must-read for the modern world."*

*—**Rolf Benirschke**,*
Former NFL Man of the Year and Health Advocate

"This book began with love – a husband's determination to help his wife feel whole again. Justin's belief in me, and his relentless search for answers, changed my life. Now it can change yours. I'm endlessly proud of him and this beautiful, important work. ♥"

—*Jodi (Jojo) Hai*

"Stress Nation *is a sharp, mission-focused guide to navigating the modern minefield of chronic stress, tech overload, and burnout. It reads like a field manual for high performers – cutting through the noise with clarity, strategy, and tools that work. If you're looking to lead, recover, and stay resilient in a world wired for overload, this book delivers.*"

—**Randy Hetrick,**
Former Navy SEAL, Founder of TRX

"*In a world where "busy" has become a badge of honor and burnout feels inevitable, Justin Hai's* Stress Nation *is the wake-up call we desperately need. With equal parts humor, heart, and hard science, Hai exposes the invisible toll technology takes on our hormones, our health, and our humanity. More than just a diagnosis of our screen-obsessed culture, this book is a roadmap to reclaiming balance, vitality, and connection. As a fellow advocate for authentic living and purposeful leadership, I'm inspired by Hai's vision – and grateful for the tools he offers to help us thrive in spite of the chaos.*"

—**Jim Fielding,**
Former Walt Disney Co., President of Disney Stores Worldwide, and author, All Pride, No Ego

STRESS NATION

JUSTIN HAI

STRESS NATION

ESCAPE THE TECHNOLOGY TRAP,
ELIMINATE STRESS, AND RECLAIM REST

WILEY

Copyright © 2025 by Justin Hai. All rights reserved.

Published by John Wiley & Sons, Inc., Hoboken, New Jersey.
Published simultaneously in Canada.

No part of this publication may be reproduced, stored in a retrieval system, or transmitted in any form or by any means, electronic, mechanical, photocopying, recording, scanning, or otherwise, except as permitted under Section 107 or 108 of the 1976 United States Copyright Act, without either the prior written permission of the Publisher, or authorization through payment of the appropriate per-copy fee to the Copyright Clearance Center, Inc., 222 Rosewood Drive, Danvers, MA 01923, (978) 750-8400, fax (978) 750-4470, or on the web at www.copyright.com. Requests to the Publisher for permission should be addressed to the Permissions Department, John Wiley & Sons, Inc., 111 River Street, Hoboken, NJ 07030, (201) 748-6011, fax (201) 748-6008, or online at http://www.wiley.com/go/permission.

The manufacturer's authorized representative according to the EU General Product Safety Regulation is Wiley-VCH GmbH, Boschstr. 12, 69469 Weinheim, Germany, e-mail: Product_Safety@wiley.com.

Trademarks: Wiley and the Wiley logo are trademarks or registered trademarks of John Wiley & Sons, Inc. and/or its affiliates in the United States and other countries and may not be used without written permission. All other trademarks are the property of their respective owners. John Wiley & Sons, Inc. is not associated with any product or vendor mentioned in this book.

Limit of Liability/Disclaimer of Warranty: While the publisher and author have used their best efforts in preparing this book, they make no representations or warranties with respect to the accuracy or completeness of the contents of this book and specifically disclaim any implied warranties of merchantability or fitness for a particular purpose. No warranty may be created or extended by sales representatives or written sales materials. The advice and strategies contained herein may not be suitable for your situation. You should consult with a professional where appropriate. Further, readers should be aware that websites listed in this work may have changed or disappeared between when this work was written and when it is read. Neither the publisher nor authors shall be liable for any loss of profit or any other commercial damages, including but not limited to special, incidental, consequential, or other damages.

For general information on our other products and services or for technical support, please contact our Customer Care Department within the United States at (800) 762-2974, outside the United States at (317) 572-3993 or fax (317) 572-4002.

Wiley also publishes its books in a variety of electronic formats. Some content that appears in print may not be available in electronic formats. For more information about Wiley products, visit our web site at www.wiley.com.

Library of Congress Cataloging-in-Publication Data is Available:

ISBN 9781394374991 (Cloth)
ISBN 9781394375004 (ePub)
ISBN 9781394375011 (ePDF)

COVER DESIGN: PAUL MCCARTHY
AUTHOR PHOTO: COURTESY OF THE AUTHOR

SKY10122988_072925

Contents

Foreword   *ix*

Introduction: How My Fascination with Cortisol Turned into a Solution for a Burned-Out, Tech-Addicted World   *xiii*

Part 1   Your Body: Cortisol, Chaos & Why You're So Damn Tired   **1**

1   Cortisol: The Hormone Running Your Life (and Ruining It)   3

2   Sleep: Nature's Reset Button—Ruined by Your Phone   25

3   Hot Flashes, Mood Swings & Midlife Mayhem? Blame Cortisol, Not Just Estrogen   47

4   Stress, Anxiety & Clickbait: The Unholy Trinity Wrecking Your Hormones   75

Part 2   Technology: How Screens Are Frying Your Brain and Your Love Life   **89**

5   Your Phone Is Smarter Than You Think—and It's Playing You   91

6   Why Kids Can't Sleep, Focus, or Play Anymore (Hint: It Glows)   113

7	**When 'Followers' Replaced Friends: Rebuilding Real Connection In Real Life**	**131**
8	**Dating Apps Are Designed to Keep You Swiping (Not Satisfied)**	**151**

Part 3   The Reset: Less Doomscrolling, More Doing   173

9	**Suck It (Literally): How Our Lozenges Help You Un-frazzle**	**175**
10	**JOMO Is the New FOMO: Outsmarting Burnout, Brain Fog & Bad Habits**	**191**
	Conclusion: From Screen Zombie to Real-Life Rockstar What Actually Works (and What to Ignore Forever)	*211*
	About the Author	*221*
	References	*223*
	Index	*239*

Foreword

You're not imagining things if you feel exhausted, unfocused, anxious, or just off. We are living through a mass dysregulation of the human brain and body. Chronic stress has rewired our physiology, and the fallout is everywhere: in our sleep, our memory, our emotions, and our health. It's not your fault; your brain isn't broken. The system is broken. You can't heal in the same environment that has created your suffering.

As a brain doctor specializing in integrative medicine, Chief Wellness Officer, and workplace wellness expert, I have spent over two decades studying the neuroscience behind stress and burnout. The results are alarming: a culture that glorifies busyness is fueling an epidemic of neuroinflammation and cortisol imbalance. In my research for *The Busy Brain Cure*, I discovered that this hormonal chaos doesn't just make us feel miserable; it reshapes our brains, our bodies, and our future.

It was during my book tour that I first met Justin Hai. From our very first conversation, it was clear: *he got it*. Grounded in science and compassion, he understood the hidden paradox that professionals miss – while technology is essential for modern life, our multi-device addiction is silently turbocharging cortisol dysregulation. His ability to connect these dots, while offering real-world solutions, immediately captured my attention.

Today, being busy and burned out is worn like a badge of honor. But the physiological reality tells a darker story. When the brain endures unrelenting stress, neuroinflammation sets in. The cortisol system – which keeps us alert, calm, and balanced – goes haywire.

Once cortisol levels become dysregulated, symptoms spiral:

- Sleepless nights that no amount of melatonin can fix.
- Memory glitches that sap confidence.
- Emotional volatility that strains relationships.
- Anxiety, depression, and a pervasive sense of exhaustion.

And for women, the stakes are even higher. In perimenopause, hormonal shifts naturally amplify cortisol imbalance. Yet most women (and too many physicians) fail to connect the dots between chronic stress, changing hormones, and worsening cognitive or emotional symptoms. Forward-thinking approaches, such as hormone replacement therapy (HRT) and other interventions that calm cortisol, could be revolutionary for restoring mental clarity, emotional resilience, and physical vitality during this critical life stage.

That's why Justin's work is vital: because it doesn't just diagnose the crisis; it dares to offer a way out. He reveals how an entire generation is stuck in survival mode, biologically hijacked by stress, and he delivers actionable, science-based strategies to interrupt the cycle – *without* abandoning the tools of modern life.

One of those tools is **Rebalance Health**, the company Justin founded. It's a supplement system rooted in the same science this book explores – designed to help regulate cortisol naturally and sustainably. In an overwhelmed world, Rebalance Health offers a practical, targeted way to restore equilibrium and help the body recover from stress at its core.

Every day, I witness the consequences of chronic cortisol overload in the workplace:

- Executive teams are paralyzed by decision fatigue.
- High-achieving women blindsided by brain fog and midlife anxiety.
- Young professionals unable to focus without a constant dopamine drip from their devices.

The truth is clear: if we don't address cortisol dysregulation at the biological level, no amount of mindfulness apps, productivity hacks, or vacations will fix the underlying problem.

This book offers hope and real healing.

It is a call to action to reset our nervous systems, recalibrate our hormones, and reclaim the health, focus, and emotional stability we've lost. We may be living through widespread physiological chaos, but it doesn't have to stay this way.

You can cure your busy brain.

But the deeper challenge is healing our culture's relationship with stress.

Stress Nation offers a blunt and much-needed starting point. In the chapters ahead, Justin makes a compelling case that real personal and societal healing begins when we confront our addiction to technology. He exposes the root issues – cortisol dysregulation – then challenges us to disconnect from our devices, restore our health and repair the emotional and relational fractures of modern life.

Turn the page. The shift from stressed-out to thriving starts here – with bold ideas, lasting solutions, and a roadmap to rebalance our bodies, our minds, and our culture.

Dr. Romie Mushtaq, MD, ABIHM
Physician | Chief Wellness Officer | Workplace Wellness Expert
Best-selling Author of *The Busy Brain Cure*

Introduction

How My Fascination with Cortisol Turned into a Solution for a Burned-Out, Tech-Addicted World

Imagine one day you are sitting on a park bench, minding your own business, when an eccentric billionaire approaches you with an offer: They'll give you 10 million dollars, right now, tax-free, for you to do whatever you wish with. The catch? You need to put your cell phone in a safety deposit box at the bank, it can't be opened until a year from now, and you can't get a new one. You'll be without a cell phone for the next 365 days, but you'll be 10 million dollars richer. You don't even have to think twice about the offer – how is this even a challenge? What's the catch?

You try to contain your smile as you nod solemnly at the mysterious figure and agree to the proposition. You walk with them to the nearest bank, power down your phone, drop it into the deposit box, sign a mountain of paperwork, and stare in awe as your account balance suddenly gains a whole lot more zeroes at the end of it.

In a daze, you shake the billionaire's hand and walk slowly out of the bank. Did that just happen? Are you a millionaire now? Not how you were expecting your day to go. Wait until your friends hear about this! You reach into your pocket to text them. Oh ... wait. Ok, that's fine, you can just call them when you get home. Do you know anyone's numbers? You know your home phone number from childhood by heart and that Tommy Tutone bop, but you can't for the life of you think of your best friend's phone number. Or your parents. Or anyone in your favorites. Email it is! People email their friends all the time, right? It's just like a slower, longer, less efficient text message. That's a totally normal way to communicate with your friends and family in the twenty-first century. Not weird at all.

This definitely needs to be on your social media, though. There's no way people are going to believe this happened to you unless you take a photo of your account balance. You head over to the ATM to grab some money, but when the account balance pops up with all those beautiful zeroes on the end and you put your face next to it, point at the screen, and … you have nothing in your hand. Can't really take a selfie without a camera. Probably for the best – you don't want everyone asking you for money anyways, right? Better keep this on a need-to-know basis.

You were on your way to work, but clearly you don't need to do that anymore – multi-millionaires don't need to work. Just a quick "I quit" to your boss on the company messaging system … nope, no access to that right now without your phone, so it looks like you'll have to quit in person. Well, that will be more satisfying and probably the professional thing to do. So, your office is downtown and you know you need to go down that street, but was it a left on Elm or a right on Birch? Your GPS app would be really helpful right now, and if everyone could just please stop honking …

Ok, fine, communication is going to be an adjustment and you're going to start to have to pay a lot better attention to navigating when you're out and about, but you're set on money for the foreseeable future. Heck, you can hire somebody to drive you from point A to point B now. You can buy one of those self-driving cars. You can buy whatever you want. What do you want? Your mind has suddenly gone blank and you can't think of anything or anywhere to shop. It'd be really nice if you could go online right now and scroll for some inspiration. You've never missed influencers and targeted ads so badly in your life before. Why is it the only thing you can think about at the moment is a new phone?

The Dark Side of Smartphones We Didn't Foresee

Giving up your smartphone is a tempting proposition that sounds much easier than it actually is. Many people, from Gen Z to Baby Boomers, don't realize just how dependent they have become on their phones for their everyday activities. Entertainment, information, communication, connection, distraction, productivity – our phones are often the first thing we look at in the morning and the last thing we see before we go to bed. Standing in line at the grocery store? Grab your phone, check those emails, and optimize your time. Waiting for friends to show up at the restaurant? Pull out your phone and scroll through social media while you're idle.

We've adapted so well to technology in our daily lives that we've forgotten how to simply exist in a place without having to occupy our time with what's on the phone in front of us. We're addicted to the glow of the screen and what each swipe might reveal. A 2022 poll (Vision Direct, n.d.) found that Americans spend an incredible 382,652 hours and 48 minutes over the average adult lifetime of 60.7 years. That equals out to almost 44 years or over half the lifetime of the average person. Screens have actually taken over our lives.

But, it wasn't always this way. The first smartphone was introduced at the turn of the millennium and quickly evolved into the miniature computers we now carry in our pockets. Since that time we've become accustomed to having the world at our fingertips – quite literally. At first, the novelty of it all was intoxicating. We went from no phones to having a phone we could talk to our loved ones on from most places in the world to having an extremely advanced piece of technology that did everything we could possibly want (and some things we probably didn't need it to).

Now, there's a growing population that longs for the days when we weren't always connected. It's as if someone hit the fast-forward button, but many of us want to rewind or even eject the tape altogether. Nostalgia for "old" media is at an all-time high from all generations, with analog tech like typewriters, film cameras, print magazines, vinyl records, and even wired headphones making a return to the mainstream.

For those that remember the days before technology was infused into every part of our lives, there's a fondness and a longing for so-called simpler times.

Instead of sitting inside and staring at a screen, kids engaged with each other and played together. There was an interactiveness to our communication because there were no screens to hide behind or escape from the world when you were out in it. When you talked to someone, you looked them in the eyes and connected on a deeper level. We had fewer choices but we never felt like we were deprived because of it.

Walking into a Blockbuster to find a video for family movie night was always an exciting proposition because you weren't sure what was going to be available and there were only so many copies of a video cassette or DVD to choose from. Nowadays you can toggle from streaming app to streaming app with hundreds of options and spend an hour without finding anything to watch. We're overloaded by choice.

Dating today feels like an impersonal game of numbers as you mindlessly swipe through an app. Before it was thrown into a high-tech algorithm, dating meant taking the time to actually get to know someone and learning about them to form a deeper relationship through emotional intimacy.

We gave our full attention to a conversation instead of multitasking our way through each meeting, glancing at our phones or outright looking at our screens mid-conversation. The irony is that while we are technically more connected today than we've ever been, we've never been more disconnected from each other.

An unexpected side effect of all these screens? We are rapidly becoming a nation of extremely stressed out, sleep-deprived individuals:

- In recent years, the American Psychiatry Association has seen increases in self-reported stress levels for their annual Healthy Minds Poll (American Psychiatric Association, 2024).
- In 2024, 43 percent of adults said that they feel more anxious than they did the previous year, which was up from 37 percent in 2023, which in turn was up from 32 percent in 2022.
- The most recent data from the Centers for Disease Control shows that inadequate sleep is on the rise, with 35.5 percent of Americans reporting they get less than seven hours of sleep per night, up from 32.3 percent in 2020 (Vision Direct, n.d.).

Much has been written about the toll that technology takes on our mental health, but many people don't know that there is a direct link between all that screen time and your physical health.

That's a lesson that I had to discover in a very personal way and is the very foundation of both this book and my life's work into studying how stress impacts the body and technology's role in that equation.

The Company That Started It All

In 2020, I co-founded Rebalance Health out of a deep curiosity about how hormones impact every aspect of our lives – from sleep and energy to focus, mood, and long-term well-being. At the time, I was exploring the world of peptides and hormone replacement therapy (HRT), but one hormone kept standing out in our research: cortisol.

Cortisol, often called the "fight or flight" hormone, has an outsized influence on how our bodies handle stress – and it became clear that this one hormone might be at the root of much of what's going wrong in modern health. Working closely with endocrinologists, holistic doctors, and integrative practitioners, we began developing ways to support healthy cortisol levels and help restore the body's natural rhythm.

That mission became deeply personal in 2021, when I watched my wife Jojo go through a brutal health journey with sleeplessness, fatigue, and intense brain fog. She was ultimately diagnosed with Cushing's syndrome, an extremely rare condition that only affects 10 to 15 people per million annually. Cushing's syndrome is a disorder that happens when the body produces too much of the hormone cortisol, commonly known as the stress hormone. However, I have dubbed it the Master Hormone because almost every cell in the human body has a cortisol receptor, so when cortisol levels are dysregulated, it affects you at every level of your being. Suddenly, all of the research and product development we'd been doing had the potential to help someone I loved more than life itself.

In Jojo's case she also sustained a severe traumatic brain injury in 1995, being pushed out of a bunk bed in her sleep by her inebriated boyfriend, falling 9 feet onto a glass coffee table, which caused the front right lobe and corpus callosum to atrophy by 25 percent and 20 percent, respectively, not to mention the unknown damage to her hypothalamus. All of which exacerbated the symptoms of Cushing's syndrome. The effects of the disease can be debilitating, causing massive mood swings, low energy, drastic weight shifts, brain fog, hot flashes, and difficulty sleeping.

Together with the Rebalance medical science team, we discovered that lowering cortisol – the body's stress signal – could unlock powerful downstream effects. Once cortisol is in balance, the body is better able to regulate estrogen and testosterone. People sleep better. Think more clearly. Feel more like themselves again.

Rebalance wasn't created for Jojo, but her experience brought the mission home in a powerful way. What started as a scientific exploration turned into a calling to help others facing similar challenges. We're living in a world that constantly pushes us out of sync – through stress, tech overload, and chronic sleep issues. We're now able to help more people rebalance their rhythm, reclaim their health, and experience more clarity, calm, and joy every day.

How to Read This Book

The way people read has changed from slogging through every word to scanning the material to see if it is worth their time to read slowly enough to take in all the nuances. Here's what I've done to make this book easy to scan:

- Chapter titles tell you what you'll learn
- Subheads are like an outline
- The most important points are bold-faced to make them easy to find.

This book has three parts.

Part 1 explains what's really going on inside your body to cause stress, plus the impacts it has on your hormones and your health.

Part 2 discusses how technology has directly affected our physiology and how we interact with each other.

Part 3 recommends what we can do to help rebalance our bodies and reset how we think about our daily technology use.

My research led me to some exceptionally talented and brilliant people who are experts in the field of hormones, sleep, technology, and menopause. You will hear from some of those people in this book as they share their insight and their recommendations to help you manage those stress-inducing pings and chimes that send your cortisol skyrocketing, while providing solutions that actually work for chronic issues like sleeplessness, hot flashes, and everyday stress.

We've conducted extensive research – grounded in science and validated by data – including multiple studies, three of which are institutional review board – approved clinical trials with medically published findings. Once I discovered a treatment protocol that actually worked – not just for my wife, but for others suffering from similar symptoms – I knew I had a responsibility to share what we had learned. This isn't hype. It's hope, backed by science, and it's helping real people reclaim their health.

Part 1
Your Body: Cortisol, Chaos & Why You're So Damn Tired

Chapter 1

Cortisol: The Hormone Running Your Life (and Ruining It)

Stress – like birth, death, and taxes – is one of those inevitable human experiences that we all must deal with. But not all stress is created equal. There's your average, everyday stress – hitting deadlines at work, bickering with our partner, trying to find the time to get everything done that we need to do in a day.

There's the more aggressive, pervasive stress – money troubles, when that bickering with your partner becomes a bigger argument that threatens the dynamics of the relationship, getting laid off from your job.

Then there is the life-threatening kind of stress – a car accident or unexpectedly coming face-to-face with an aggressive wild animal while out on a nature hike. Everyone copes with stress differently and everyone has a different threshold for how much stress they can realistically handle before they hit their emotional limit.

Let's suspend reality for a moment, and put yourself in the position of Woody Harrelson's character David Murphy in the early 1990s hit erotic drama *Indecent Proposal*. You know the one, where Robert Redford's character offers one million dollars for one night with Demi Moore. For this thought experiment, you'll have to put aside the extremely problematic undertones of women as property that were rampant in pop culture during that decade.

Desperate for money to save your dream home after a recession wipes away your finances and job, you head to Vegas to strike it rich by gambling with the last of your savings. Predictably, you lose it all. Less predictably, a mysterious stranger with Robert Redford's good looks and none of your money problems suddenly takes an interest in your wife and offers you a fortune to spend the night with her.

You refuse, but are later talked into the proposition by said wife.

Again, predictably, you have a change of heart in a spectacularly dramatic fashion that leads to you trying to chase them down and stop the encounter, only to miss the departing helicopter. I told you we were suspending reality, remember?

Unlikely scenario as it is, it's a very poignant example of someone dealing with an abundance of stress – the stress of losing a job, a home, money, and now the added strain of a high roller swooping in to seduce your partner on their private yacht.

That's the snowball effect at work leading to a series of less-than-stellar decisions after hitting the limit of life-altering stressful situations that one person can take.

Stress is one of the most basic instincts our bodies have, which is because it's tied directly to our survival instincts. When our body is faced with a type of stress – be it physical, emotional or mental – our body releases hormones that prepare us to protect ourselves or make a beeline for the nearest safe exit. It's a mini – survival response that you have no control over – when you see a perceived threat or are startled suddenly, even though you logically know that you are most likely not in any real danger, your body reverts to our caveman ancestors mindset of "Oh no, a bear! Run away!".

Never mind the fact that odds are good there isn't actually a bear in front of you that you are responding to. Your body responds to all stress – be it minor inconveniences at work to actual life-threatening danger – with the same physiological response. It's why you have the same ratcheting up of your heart rate when you get a "call me" text from your mother with zero context as you do when someone cuts you off suddenly on the highway.

Our bodies don't check in and ask our brains if a threat is logical in times of crisis – we survive by reacting quickly to perceived threats.

The hormone partially responsible for that quick response is called cortisol, a.k.a. The Stress Hormone, and the response is commonly referred to as the "fight or flight" response.

Why Cortisol Is the Master Hormone

While the name "Stress Hormone" isn't exactly untrue, it's not a term I actually agree with due to its extremely unflattering nature. It implies that cortisol is a negative influence on your body, causing you to freak out and panic at every tiny provocation. But **cortisol is actually so much more than just stress,** and it's not a completely uncontrollable hormone. In fact, **almost every molecule in the body has a cortisol receptor, controlling everything from your metabolism to your sleep cycle.** It's why I've decided to become cortisol's personal hype man and help it rebrand itself as the "Master Hormone."

Now, if you read hormone and immediately got confused, that's understandable. For many people, the only hormones they are aware of are the ones that go haywire when puberty hits, causing them to be whirling dervishes of nervous, moody, awkward, sexually frustrated energy that take risks with very little concept of consequences in a burning desire to be accepted by their peers – a.k.a. teenagers. However, **your sex hormones aren't the only hormones that are produced by the body.**

In fact, **scientists have identified 50 hormones in the body** so far, each created by a different organ or system in the body with a unique purpose that is imperative for helping you function each day.

In simple terms, **hormones are chemicals that work by transmitting a message through the blood to signal to your body to do a certain function and specify when exactly to do that function.** These hormones and the organs and glands that create and release them make up what is called your endocrine system.

Testosterone, estrogen, and progesterone are all examples of sex hormones, which are released by the ovaries and testes to control our reproductive cycles; however, **your brain contains multiple glands responsible for releasing hormones** like dopamine (the "Happy Hormone") and oxytocin (the "Huggy Hormone") – clearly they both had better PR agents when scientists were giving out nicknames).

Some organs, which are not technically part of the endocrine system, are also part of this hormone-releasing cycle – your liver, for instance, which releases an insulin-like growth factor, or even your gastrointestinal tract, which releases GLP-1, a hormone that regulates appetite, blood sugar, and digestion. Yes, the same GLP-1 that is currently being targeted via drugs like Ozempic.

As science learns more about our hormones and their functions in the body, we're also learning more about how to optimize those systems and solve many common and long-standing issues – hormones truly are essential for our daily health and functions.

If that sounds like more biology than you bargained for, think of your body like an office, with cortisol as an extremely nervous and easily startled project manager. Your cortisol keeps everything on track and running smoothly to get the job done and keep the client happy.

When it is balanced and working at its optimal capacity, everybody is happy and getting out of work on time, being nice to each other, taking proper lunch breaks, and generally getting along and enjoying their lives.

When it is out of balance, it's pure chaos, with everyone pulling late nights, stealing each other's leftovers out of the office fridge, running around screaming at each other, trash cans inexplicably on fire, until someone finally rams the printer through the conference room glass wall and walks out smoking a cigarette while the sprinkler system kicks on and Debbie from Accounting cries under her desk. In other words, it's not good.

Cortisol, the true multitasker of the endocrine system, is produced by your adrenal glands, which are small triangular-shaped glands that are located on top of each of your kidneys. Your adrenal glands are also responsible for producing a handful of other hormones, like adrenaline (more on that later), androgens (a.k.a. male sex hormones like testosterone present in both men and women), and estrogen.

As Alison Gracom, PA-C, an endocrinology expert, explains it, cortisol is a multifaceted hormone because it truly has an effect on so many of your body's systems, both in positive and negative ways. **"Cortisol has a rhythm – we always start high in the morning and have peaks and troughs throughout the day,"** she explains, "with your global peak in the morning and your lowest trough late at night." This is especially important because **cortisol regulates our sleep-wake cycle**, which we'll talk more about in Chapter 2.

Gracom also notes that **cortisol actually increases the body's production of glucose and raises our blood pressure, which is directly tied to that sleep–wake cycle.** "It's stimulating you to get up in the morning, feeding your body, to a degree, raising your blood pressure, waking up your brain to get up and go," she says.

Cortisol has a direct impact on your metabolism, controlling how you use fats, protein, and carbohydrates for energy. It can also help lower inflammation and boost your immune response, when it's functioning at proper levels in that ebb and flow cycle. **It's a steroid hormone that affects every cell of your body – from your bones to your heart to your reproductive system to your skin, hair, and nails.**

Cortisol, explains Gracom, is life-sustaining – you need it to function and without it you could become weak, fatigued, and lose an unhealthy amount of weight. But, on the flip side of that coin, like many things that make us feel good in life – say, chocolate cake or trashy reality television – too much of a good thing can very quickly make you sick. In the case of cortisol, quite literally.

Cortisol in its healthy state is meant to go up and down with the normal "rest and digest" range throughout the day and exceed normal levels in appropriate situations. For our caveman ancestors, cortisol in an elevated state is an alarm system – that "fight or flight" response that kept them alive in a world filled with predators wanting to make them the meal of the day. We definitely have moments where that alarm system is needed – driving our car and having to dodge someone who runs a red light, sensing an unfamiliar person following us too closely or for too long, smelling smoke in the middle of the night – that works in tandem with adrenaline (another product of the adrenal glands) to help us survive.

When Cortisol Gets Stuck on High

Adrenaline is triggered by cortisol – when cortisol has a dramatic spike very quickly from one of those scary situations, that's adrenaline's cue. As Gracom puts it, that "oh shit" moment gets cortisol to skyrocket, which is the hormone's way to say that it is sensing danger and telling adrenaline to release to encourage your body to act.

Cortisol is the alarm, adrenaline is the action.

If a burglar was breaking into your home, cortisol would spike to set off your alarm system, while adrenaline would then tell your body to either get up and grab a baseball bat or jump out the bedroom window to run away.

But, adrenaline also takes a lot out of your body, so it's not triggered every time that cortisol level gets high – only when there is a sudden, dramatic spike.

Adrenaline causes your body to consolidate its functions and conserve and expend to only the most necessary for survival in that moment. It doesn't heighten all of your senses, so you lose certain ones in the moment, like hearing or peripheral vision. It redirects blood flow to your vital organs, meaning your other organs don't have blood flow as the crisis is happening.

Coming down from an adrenaline spike is not a fun situation, as anyone who has ever experienced one knows – you wind up feeling exhausted, shaky, and fully and completely spent. Think of your worst hangover from college and then times that by 10.

But, adrenaline lets the human body do some pretty amazing things. You've likely heard stories of mothers who are able to push cars to save their children or normal people scaling walls to escape certain death. Adrenaline and cortisol can make us into literal superheroes for a moment in time, helping us protect ourselves and our loved ones when the moment calls for it. Sure, we'll feel like absolute crap after the fact, but it's pretty amazing what the human body is capable of when it senses actual danger.

Fortunately for us, adrenaline only comes into the picture after dramatic spikes of cortisol – it's not something that we need to worry about jacking up our system every time we get one of those "Hey, can we talk messages" from our manager. But that doesn't mean that raised cortisol levels don't have an impact on your long-term health.

In fact, according to Gracom, **sustained, high levels of cortisol can actually lead to chronic, long-term health problems.** Basically, you can stress yourself out so much that you actually make yourself sick. This is the difference between dealing with occasional, healthy stress responses to normal triggers and being chronically stressed out.

If you are constantly having these cortisol peaks for a prolonged period of time, multiple days in a row, it's not going to be good for your health – physically or mentally. You're basically living in a state of constant stress, unable to return to a point of stasis or hit those cortisol lows that even you out and keep you calm. And the effects on your body will not be short-term effects, like adrenaline surges – they compound over time and can lead to long-term ones that affect your whole system in ways that might surprise you.

"High cortisol can raise your glucose to the point of diabetes," says Gracom. "It can actually start affecting your cells and how you process glucose." Remember those GLP-1 hormones we talked about earlier? Well, prolonged cortisol spikes can actually disable so-called glucose transporters inside the cells, which makes medications ineffective against it, including weight loss meds designed to target GLP-1, like Ozempic, she says.

Prolonged cortisol peaks can cause inflammation, lower your immune response, and even, notes Gracom, destroy brain tissue, according to studies in both children and adults (Wiedenmayer et al., 2006).

Think about that – **being stressed out is literally making us lose critical parts of our brain like memory and our ability to process and regulate our emotions.** Those are extremely important functions for day-to-day life and generally existing as a happy, healthy, well-adjusted human.

How angry would you be if you were unable to remember a memory that brought you a lot of joy because you were so stressed out working on a project at work that had absolutely no importance to you personally? Odds are good you'd be pretty upset – and the kicker is, **all that stress means you most likely wouldn't**

be very good at regulating that anger, because the stress had impacted your ability to healthily deal with your emotions. Talk about a catch-22.

Our caveman ancestors had plenty to stress about, what with the giant cave bears and having to find shelter and hunt and gather to survive. But, from what we understand about their lives, they weren't suffering from cortisol imbalances and generalized anxiety. Granted, I don't think cave psychiatry was big back in the prehistoric days, but it's hard to have an existential crisis about the state of the world when you're just trying to figure out if you can survive until the next day. And yet, despite all the very real stressors they faced, **the concept of constant, daily, sustained stress is a thoroughly modern problem.** I'd argue it's a problem many of us didn't really deal with until the twenty-first century.

We Used to Have Endings

Before the 2000s, there was no shortage of stress; however, it felt contained. Our lives were not 24/7 – everything had a clear ending. Our jobs were truly 9 a.m. to 5 p.m. and then we went home and didn't worry about them until the next day.

Even our entertainment had a stopping point as televisions would end their broadcasting at midnight. Want to watch TV until the wee hours of the morning because you can't sleep? Well, too bad – there are only three major networks and they go off the air at midnight with the sounding of a patriotic national anthem paired to the visual of the stars and stripes waving in the breeze followed by static. So unless you found static amusing (no judgment), it was time to turn off the TV and head to bed.

There was no cable news with talking heads spending hours picking apart every angle of an issue with breathless importance, riling you up over a topic you didn't know you were supposed to be emotionally invested in, but now are somehow very stressed out about.

There was no expectation that you would be available after hours, or while away on vacation, or while you were sick, or during your parental leave. Mostly because there was no real way for your co-workers to reach you when you were out of the office – out of the office truly meant out of the office.

Cortisol and the Loss of Endings

I think you can guess what the tipping point was that changed all this – technology. As tech became more advanced and we became more connected, suddenly our stress and anxiety levels skyrocketed (Fioroni and Foy, 2025).

We started sleeping less, which contributed to the problem.

As Todd Dorfman, MD, a physician specializing in hormone management and Rebalance chief medical officer notes, **cortisol levels go down during sleep, meaning cortisol is important for hormone rebalancing.** "It's almost like you're rebooting your brain when you sleep," he explains, a topic we'll talk more in depth about in the next chapter, as **sleep, like cortisol, is one of the secrets to maintaining your body's emotional, physical, and mental stability.**

But, **technology, with its rapid evolution and addictive nature, swept in and knocked our systems for a loop.** We might as well have been our troglodyte cousins for all that we were prepared for what devices like the smartphone were doing to our brains and bodies.

Once social media entered the picture, we had no real way to understand the impact it would have on us, and we're only now beginning to see the damage its wreaking on children and teens, with chronically online kids unable to socialize in real life and dealing with anxiety and self-esteem issues at younger and younger ages.

If that sounds dismal, it's because it is, but **it's important to note the correlation between technology, sleep, and cortisol over the last two decades.** We've become a nation of stressed out, overworked, screen zombies and it's making us physically sick.

Think about the last time you and a friend got together. During that catch-up, odds are good that one of you asked the other how you were doing. It tends to be a thing that friends do when they chat. And, odds are equally as good that the other person responded with something along the lines of tired, busy, or stressed out. It's become our default state of being. We're rarely good, or calm, or happy or content.

We're treading water while someone keeps attaching weights to our arms. Sometimes it almost feels like a one-upmanship to see who has the most dysfunction in their daily life. That if you aren't busy or stressed or tired then perhaps you aren't succeeding and need to work harder.

If you are enjoying yourself and have time to relax or leave work on time then you clearly are underachieving and not reaching your full potential, right?

We have so many tools at our disposal to maximize our output and be more efficient, to capitalize on every waking moment, that if you are taking time to just sit quietly with your thoughts or be present in nature, you must not be the type of person with the drive to succeed in the modern world.

We've created artificial intelligence tools, not to help us solve complex problems that are outside the realm of human understanding, or to help uncomplicate our lives so that we can be less stressed, but to create "art" and be "creative" – tasks that normally function as ways for us to relieve stress and sort through complicated emotions.

13

Cortisol: The Hormone Running Your Life (and Ruining It)

Somewhere along the way, we collectively agreed that we needed to be more. That in order to live an exceptional life, we needed to maximize our output. If there are 24 hours in a day, we should be making the most of each and every one of them. The "I'll sleep when I'm dead mentality," with every hour accounted for as an hour to be utilized. Or the, "I get up every day at 4 a.m. and accomplish more before 9 a.m. than most people do all day," CEO.

Do you ever sit and just be present in a moment – not thinking about everything you need to do, or looking at a screen of some sort – but just sitting in a moment and appreciating it for what it is?

Many of us have lost that ability, unable to do so much as stand in line at the grocery story without checking our emails or texting someone. Which might not sound like a big deal, until you realize that **every time you look at that screen, there's a potential cortisol spike waiting to happen,** keeping you in that sustained peak state that Gracom warns is a chronic health risk to so many of your vital systems.

Cortisol Overload Is the New Normal

We've been living in this stress state for so long that many of us have just accepted it, or, even worse, it doesn't even register on our internal radars that we're just constantly stressed. Our bodies, on the other hand, are acutely aware. Chronic pain sufferers know they are in pain, but it isn't until the pain is addressed and they no longer feel it every day that they realize just how bad they truly felt and how much it impacted their lives and their ability to enjoy themselves.

Take, for example, teeth grinding (stay with me here). Also known as bruxism, it was a relatively common issue before the pandemic, with scientists estimating somewhere around 31 percent of adults were chronically grinding their teeth (Manfredini et al., 2013).

Fast-forward to a few years post-pandemic after the lockdowns were lifted and many clinics were reporting almost three times as many patients showing up to their practices with signs of clenching and grinding (Weiss, 2022). Bruxism, according to dentists, has always been linked to stress and anxiety, and in the first few months that followed the lockdowns, Google searches for teeth grinding, bruxism, and clenching skyrocketed (Kardeş and Kardeş, 2021).

Unconsciously (and, for some, consciously), many of us were transferring the stress of a global pandemic into our teeth, clenching and gnashing all that uncertainty into our jaws. A night guard can only handle so much, friends.

Cortisol, Stress, and Insulin Resistance

Then there's your gastrointestinal system, a.k.a. your gut. The gut is a very delicate ecosystem and when you're stressed, it lets you know it's none too happy with the situation. Some of that goes back to the glucose production that Gracom was mentioning earlier.

In an ideal world, where you are reaching those peaks and troughs, cortisol is helping in the release of glucose to help raise your blood sugar and produce energy. Which is perfect because you need that energy to get you through yet another boring Zoom meeting.

But, if you are in a constant state of stress with elevated cortisol, your body doesn't stop pumping glucose into the blood, even when you've hit the amount that you need, which in turn keeps your blood sugar high and eventually could make your cells resistant to insulin (Cleveland Clinic, 2025).

That's significant because insulin's job is to move the glucose in the bloodstream into your cells, converting it into energy. **With heightened cortisol, your pancreas will keep pumping out that insulin in an effort to convert the glucose in the bloodstream to energy, but your body won't respond to it because of the**

constant stream of glucose hitting your blood that the cortisol keeps pumping out. It creates a vicious cycle of high blood sugar and insulin resistance. Some people could even develop Type 2 diabetes if this cycle continues.

High Cortisol Leads to Heartburn

If you are someone who suffers from gastroesophageal reflux disease (GERD), commonly known as acid reflux, cortisol directly affects acid reflux and heartburn. For the uninitiated, GERD simply means the lower esophageal sphincter muscle (there's a fun muscle), which acts as a type of door between your stomach and your esophagus, doesn't work properly, allowing acids to rise up from the stomach and into the esophagus. When you are stressed, you produce more stomach acid, hence more instances of acid reflux (Golen and Ricciotti, 2022). When I said earlier that cortisol was the Master Hormone, I wasn't being facetious – it truly affects and controls so many different systems.

Now, this is the time when some of you might be thinking to yourself, I don't want my body to react like this. How can I just remove myself from stress altogether and live a so-called "stress-free" life? And, in theory, the idea of sequestering yourself away to some remote location – a serene tropical island; a quiet cabin in the woods; a Mars colony, whenever that becomes a thing – and surrounding yourself with only the things that make you happy does sound like an idyllic way to live. Just removing everything that causes you stress, from work to money to family drama and just staying at this calm plateau with no unnecessary cortisol spikes.

Or, perhaps you've done the lite version of that with the "disconnecting" vacation where you unplug your devices or stay off social media because you know that technology triggers your stress levels.

If stress makes us feel bad, then no stress should make us feel good, right? Sadly, no.

"I think what's lost on some people is that the peaks are just as important as the troughs," Gracom says, meaning the highs are equally as important as the lows. "If you're eating sweets all day long, it doesn't taste so sweet anymore, right? If you feel happy all the time, do you really recognize happiness? You need sorrow to make happiness so much sweeter. The troughs are just as important – they are vital."

In order for your body to function optimally, it must have both the highs and the lows of cortisol, the peaks and the troughs, otherwise your body can't regulate those systems.

Even if you are the calmest and most even-natured person on the planet, your cortisol will eventually rise because you will at some point experience a stress occurrence that causes that alarm system to go off. Maybe your peaceful mountain cabin experiences an unexpected guest in the form of a bear. Or maybe your tropical island getaway has a not-so-peaceful tropical storm. Or perhaps your futuristic Mars space retreat has a major malfunction with your water reclaimer (that seems like a thing that could happen to a Mars space house, right?).

Whatever the catalyst, there will always be something that will happen that will add an unexpected stress event to your life and cause either that dramatic, adrenaline-releasing spike of cortisol or a regular, everyday peak of cortisol.

Not to mention the fact that cortisol levels naturally fluctuate throughout the day as part of our circadian rhythm – that's our natural design and it's how our body knows when it's time to get up and go for the day and when it's time to stop and rest.

If your cortisol didn't have those peaks and troughs, your circadian rhythm wouldn't properly function and your sleep cycle would be out of alignment.

Cushing's Syndrome and Addison's Disease

A very small percentage of the population don't experience those peaks and troughs.

There are two rare hormonal disorders that are directly linked to cortisol: Cushing's syndrome and Addison's disease.

For those with Cushing's, the adrenal glands make too much cortisol. This can lead to a variety of symptoms that include everything from weight gain to high blood pressure to fatigue to easy bruising of the skin. Cushing also can lead to bone loss, making your bones easily broken. It's been linked to depression, anxiety, memory loss, sleeplessness, headaches, and emotions that are difficult to control. Sound familiar? It's all the issues we've touched on that come with sustained cortisol spikes, but at a much more serious and debilitating level.

Cushing affects about 10–15 people per million, making it an extremely rare condition.

Addison's disease, on the other hand, is when the adrenal glands do not produce enough cortisol. Instead of going into a fight or flight reaction in times of stress or danger, you instead become confused or lethargic. Symptoms can include extreme fatigue, weight loss, loss of appetite, low blood sugar, nausea, muscle and joint pain, depression, irritability, low blood pressure, fainting, and areas of darkened skin. Many of the symptoms overlap with Cushing's syndrome, making it hard to distinguish between the two.

Addison's disease is estimated to affect 40 and 60 people per million, meaning it is yet another rare hormone disorder.

While both are treatable, it takes time and lots of testing and trial and error to find the right combination of medication to help counteract that imbalance.

It just goes to highlight how important cortisol is to our bodies' daily functions and why living in a constant state of stress should not be the status quo.

Cortisol, Aging, and Menopause

One function of cortisol that many people don't talk about is its role in the aging process. As Gracom points out, cortisol is needed to help secrete the growth hormone – imperative for both children, to reach their healthy height and to build bone density, and adults, to help maintain youth and build muscle mass (Stratatkis, 2006).

However, notes Gracom, **if your cortisol levels go too high for too long of a period, you actually stop making the growth hormone.** As an adult, that's not great if you like, say, looking youthful and having lean muscle mass, but the issue gets worse once you start hitting your 40s, 50s, and 60s – especially if you are a person with a uterus and ovaries. That's because of a little something called menopause.

While cortisol isn't necessarily directly impacted by menopause in terms of it being a hormone that drops off in production like estrogen, progesterone, and testosterone, this natural life cycle is intertwined with cortisol in a few different ways that we'll discuss more in Chapter 3.

But what anyone who is getting a little longer in the tooth knows is that as you age, your sleep is one of the first things that begins to suffer. For women, menopause tends to be the main factor due to symptoms like hot flashes and night sweats; however, increased stress plays a role for everyone.

Your 40s and 50s are typically your highest-earning years – you tend to be in a senior level role with the most responsibilities you will have at work. You might be managing multiple people and be seen as someone to go to when there is a crisis – and, let's be real, there's always a crisis.

At home, this is the time when your family life is changing in meaningful ways. Those with children are experiencing or about to experience an empty nest as kids depart for college.

Some women in their 40s might just be starting a family or choosing to have another child – an option that wasn't as common or a possibility for many but that scientific advances have helped to make a reality.

Or, on the opposite end of the spectrum, you might be dealing with the stress of a boomerang child who moves back in to save on finances in an increasingly more expensive world. That, in turn, can add additional stress to you and on your marriage, if you have a partner.

If you are approaching retirement years, you may be stressing about your finances and if you have enough to live comfortably and support yourself and the type of life you want to live in your golden years.

And, if you have aging parents, you could be filling the role of a full-time caretaker or handling arrangements for their medical care.

It all kind of makes you nostalgic for those bygone, carefree-by-comparison days of your 20s and 30s. Not enough to make you want to relive those decades and go through all that uncertainty and youthful drama, but many of the issues you faced back then can seem almost quaint in comparison. Plus, your knees still had all their cartilage and your neck wasn't constantly freezing up every time you slept on it a certain way, so that was a big plus.

The point being, there are plenty of very real and unique challenges that come with age and they can all impact your cortisol at a time when you are already dealing with some pretty significant biological changes to your hormones that impact your sleep. And, as we now know, when your sleep is affected, your cortisol is thrown out of rhythm, leading to even more cortisol imbalance for a self-perpetuating cycle.

It's no wonder that cortisol is slowly becoming a trending topic in wellness circles, with more and more so-called solutions to combating elevated cortisol hitting the market every day.

Unfortunately, what the majority of those products miss, says Gracom, is they either don't have the correct blend of adaptogens and botanicals to have the right effect on cortisol, or they aren't using a delivery system that gets those botanicals to your system to have an impact on your cortisol rhythms.

I've seen all of this firsthand with Jojo – when her diagnosis came through, I searched high and low for a treatment that could help regulate her cortisol, but every supplement made promises it could not scientifically deliver on.

Why I Created Rebalance Health – And What Makes It Unique

It's why we worked to find the best combination of ingredients and delivery method that would eventually become Rebalance Health's products. **Not only does Rebalance Health provide the adaptogens, herbs, and botanicals that are scientifically tested and proven** to help encourage your body to find that proper circadian rhythm (the 24-hour sleep–wake cycle that our system runs on), but it **delivers via a method that actually ensures those ingredients make it into the body.**

The majority of supplements simply go through the digestive system and the nutrients are not absorbed by the body – that's why you see such astronomical percentages like 1,000 percent daily value on many vitamin labels. You're not going to actually get that with a product because the majority of the ingredients are going to be destroyed by your digestive system before they have a chance to get into your bloodstream where they can have an impact. It's why Americans have some of the most expensive pee in the world – the ingredients in their supplements have not been made bioavailable.

It's one thing to know that, say ashwagandha is an effective adaptogenic herb for helping to relieve stress, but throwing it into a pressed pill and thinking taking it once a day will have a noticeable effect on your cortisol is like thinking there's a magic Botox pill that will make you look 10 years younger. If you believe that, I know a bridge in Brooklyn that I can sell you for a great price.

Technology Addiction Is the Problem. Cortisol Balance Is the Solution

If there's one thing I want you to take away from this chapter it's that cortisol is not the bogeyman that can be blamed for everything bad in life. The Fed raises interest rates and cortisol is at fault. You get in a fender bender and your cortisol somehow did it.

Cortisol is a hormone that is necessary for life. We cannot survive without it. Where things go wrong with cortisol is when our systems go haywire – be it from sustained, high periods of stress caused by our continuously connected lives keeping us perpetually plugged in and always on alert, or when we can't sleep and our circadian rhythm is thrown for a loop. Oftentimes the former is a contributing factor to the latter.

But it's not cortisol's fault – **cortisol imbalance is the symptom of a larger health epidemic that can be traced back to our addiction to technology.** You need cortisol to be, as Gracom puts it, your gas and brakes for the day, to tell your body when it's time to go and when it's time to slow down and rest.

Now that you understand exactly how important cortisol is to your body, it's time to dive into an issue that affects billions of people worldwide and will not only make you extremely cranky and unpopular with anyone in your immediate vicinity, but will also severely mess with that precious cortisol rhythm – not getting enough sleep.

Resource

Sign up for this free educational email course at www.StressNationBook.com: "The Perimenopause Survival Blueprint: The 5 Biggest Mistakes Women Make When Dealing with Hot Flashes That Lead to Sleepless Nights, Fears of Losing Their Marriage Due to Loss of Sexual Desire, and Brain Fog So Bad They Can't Do Their Job (Plot Twist: The Problem Is Cortisol, Not Estrogen).

- Day 1: The mistake almost every woman makes when she thinks "this is just aging"
- Day 2: The hidden habits that spike cortisol and sabotage sleep
- Day 3: Why your libido is down – and it's not just hormones or age
- Day 4: What brain fog really is, and how to clear it without caffeine or willpower
- Day 5: The real reason so many women don't improve (even with the "right" supplements) – and how to fix it.

Chapter 2

Sleep: Nature's Reset Button—Ruined by Your Phone

In 2010, candy bar company Mars launched a now iconic commercial for its candy bar Snickers featuring the legendary Betty White getting very physical and trash talking while playing a not-so-friendly game of football. The spot culminated with her being given a chocolate bar and transforming back into the football playing bro she actually was. The infamous tagline, "You're not you when you're hungry" was born. The ads continued throughout the next decade, swapping in celebrities like Willem Dafoe, Liza Minnelli, Danny Trejo, and Joe Pesci.

While memorable and culturally significant (and extremely entertaining), I'd argue the sentiment behind that tagline should instead be applied to sleep, because **you truly are not you when you're sleep-deprived.**

If you've ever had been stuck in an airport after a day of cascading flight delays and cancellations, or pulled an ill-advised all-nighter trying to complete a project at the last minute, or, you know, had kids, you are extremely familiar with the disorienting sensation of true, bone-deep exhaustion and what it can do to the mind and body.

Being cranky is not just for toddlers who miss their nap time **when you don't get the sleep your body needs, your brain**

is not able to emotionally regulate, resulting in extreme reactions to situations that a well-rested you would typically be able to handle with a level head. It's why you can feel overwhelmed and frustrated by simple tasks that typically would be manageable on your standard sleep schedule, or turn into a much angrier version of yourself when someone does something to aggravate you when normally you'd just let it slide.

There's a reason sleep deprivation is used as a form of advanced interrogation – not sleeping for days can make your mind a confusing, complicated jumble where down is up, cold is hot, and you have no idea why your keys are in the refrigerator and the sour cream is in the medicine cabinet.

Everyone knows that they aren't themselves when they're tired (I'm telling you, you're not you when you're tired is the better ad campaign – hangry doesn't have anything on exhausted), but have you ever stopped to think about why that is?

Hormones Require Sleep to Be Replenished

There's more going on than just being so ridiculously tired that your brain forgets how to do simple tasks. In fact, on a physiological level, sleep is the ultimate Ctrl + Alt + Delete for your system, helping your body and your mind hit reset for the day ahead. But, it's not just your mind that is getting a recharge – **your body also uses this time to produce the hormones that you need for the day ahead, including cortisol.**

When you get enough sleep, you are able to replenish your cortisol levels and ensure they are at the proper levels when you awake in the morning. If you don't get enough sleep, you are more likely to have an imbalance of cortisol, which will in turn make you have a disproportionate response to any stress you encounter that day and will make it harder for you to both wake up in the morning and fall asleep later that night.

As you sleep, you go through a variety of restorative processes in practically every cell of your body, while your mind uses that time to process emotions and complex problems that you faced during your day. It's a delicate balance, and if you're not getting good, quality sleep (key word there is quality – not all sleep is created equal) then you are setting yourself up to have a very challenging day, to say the least.

When we sleep, our bodies and minds take time to not only process and repair our systems from what happened during the day, but it's also when our brains and bodies prepare themselves for the following day. That includes resetting your cortisol levels, which you now know is a crucial hormone for regulating everything from your metabolism to your immune system.

Throughout your sleep cycle, your body is slowly revving up cortisol production from its lowest point at bedtime to ensure it is at its optimum peak when you wake up in the morning – your gas for the day to get you going.

Breakfast might be the most important meal of the day, but **if you are sleep-deprived, there's no amount of coffee and Wheaties that are going to pep you up and course correct if your cortisol for the day is out of whack.** Instead, you'll be on edge and disproportionately stressed out and agitated. Not the healthy start to the day you envisioned.

You've been told how important a good night's sleep is for your mental and physical health, but odds are good you don't know exactly why that is. In this chapter, we'll take a deeper look at:

- What's happening to your body while you're dreaming
- The real reason it's so important to get a good night's rest

Sleep: Nature's Reset Button—Ruined by Your Phone

- How our technology addiction can interfere with our natural circadian rhythm
- The lengths that we go to get better sleep
- Why most of those methods don't actually do much, and
- What you can do to improve your sleep quantity and quality

Understanding Sleep

Sleep might sound like a very simple concept: You're tired, so you go to bed and you wake up refreshed and ready to start a new day. But, **while you are unconscious there's an entire complex system of recovery and rebooting happening** at the very cellular level of your being. In order for that to happen without a hitch, you need to both get the proper amount of rest, and the right type of rest.

    Depending on your age, every person needs certain hours of sleep every night to operate at the optimum mental, emotional, and physical peak. According to the National Sleep Foundation, that means between 8 to 10 hours for teenagers, 7 to 9 hours for adults aged 18 to 64, and between 7 and 8 hours for adults over the age of 65 (National Sleep Foundation, 2024). And no, napping does not count as part of that total – we're talking uninterrupted, consecutive hours of sleep at a specified time of the day.

The Best Times to Sleep and Wake for Healthy Cortisol Levels

One of the best things about being a grown-up is going to bed whenever the heck you want, right? Well, about that – as Alison Gracom, PA-C, our resident cortisol expert notes, you might not have a bedtime, but your body sure does. That's because your body follows what is called a natural circadian rhythm or a 24-hour cycle that is synchronized to the light-to-dark cycle. Studies have shown that **cortisol is at its lowest in the 11 p.m. to midnight** timeframe (Chan and Debono, 2010), meaning that is the absolute latest you should be going to bed in order to not disrupt your natural cortisol cycle (sorry, night owls). It's your natural brakes on the machine that is your body. **Cortisol peaks at around 8 a.m. to 9 a.m.,** which is your body's way of saying get up and start your day – the aforementioned gas for your system to get you moving.

And no, **you can't fudge that timeline by getting the proper amount of sleep at a different time of day.** "There's this assumption of 'If I go to bed at 2 a.m. but I sleep until 10 a.m., therefore I'm healthy,'" says Gracom. "It's not true. We find the later you go to bed, the higher the cortisol sustains." It throws off your natural rhythm and a disease state can kick in.

"One of the things we look at for medical disease is how high your cortisol is at bedtime," Gracom explains. "We'll do a salivary cortisol test and if that cortisol is over the 0.09 threshold at bedtime, that's a sign of actual disease state."

Gracom points to the numerous studies that have been conducted focusing on night shift workers that show despite getting the same amount of sleep as those on a day shift, the night crew tended to suffer from higher levels of cardiovascular disease, obesity, reproductive and gastrointestinal dysfunction, and even cancer (Eastman and Smith, 2012).

In fact, the International Agency for Research on Cancer (IARC) found the results of many of these studies to be so compelling that they designated night shift work as "probably carcinogenic to humans." (IARC, 2020).

Kind of makes you rethink staying up extra late to binge watch whatever show your sleep-deprived brain thought it needed to stare at a screen until 4 a.m. to finish. Those of us that remember the days of the TV broadcast turning itself to snow at midnight on the dot can be grateful to the television networks for forcing us to go to bed – hard to stay up all night staring at a screen when there's literally nothing on it.

You Can't Make Up for Lost Sleep

As you've probably guessed, that also means the idea of making up for a "sleep debt" also is not a real thing. Sorry, but there's no reasoning with your internal alarm clock, no matter how much you try to logic the issue.

For those unfamiliar with the term, the idea around sleep debt is that if you only get 4 hours of sleep tonight, then you try and "make up" for the sleep you didn't get by sleeping for 10 hours to cover the deficit of 3 hours you missed the night before. But, as we now know, cortisol is a bit of a brat in that it doesn't really care that you didn't sleep the night before and you want to be good tonight and bank more sleep to help make up the difference.

Your circadian cycle is already set and your cortisol production was determined long ago by evolution to be tied to that light–dark cycle, technology and the responsibilities and diversions of the modern world be damned. Our caveman ancestors probably didn't have much of a nightlife to keep them up past their optimal bedtime, but society and technology have evolved at a lightspeed pace compared to the human body.

Why Your Body Needs a Regular Sleep Schedule

In fact, there's evidence to prove that sleeping too much is actually detrimental to your health and cognitive function. There's a reason sleep hygiene suggests going to bed and getting up at the same time every day – studies have shown that too much sleep also throws off your circadian rhythm, working in much the same way as too little sleep, says Dr. Dorfman. **"You're relying on melatonin secretion at night to help you get to sleep, and cortisol secretion in the morning to help you wake up"** he explains. "All of that gets discombobulated when you sleep too little or too much – they're very similar."

He points to a process called synaptic pruning, which is basically your brain selectively "forgetting" certain things while you sleep. "It's how you get rid of the day-to-day memories, the anxiety, consolidate short-term into long-term, decide what to remember and what to forget – basically get rid of the garage and detoxify your brain," says Dr. Dorfman.

Studies have shown that with too little sleep, the brain isn't able to play gardener and prune those connections, meaning you wake up with a jumble in your mind and your cognitive function and memory are a total crapshoot for the day ahead.

Interestingly enough, the same thing happens for those who get too much sleep, as the circadian rhythm is out of balance. It's a case of same same, but different – same problem, different cause. And while forgetting where you left your keys (hint, probably in your pants' pocket or the bottom of your purse … again) is annoying, **missing out on that synaptic pruning can potentially lead to long-term effects.** Recent studies have shown a link between sleep disturbances and the risk for Alzheimer's, particularly in women (Yale School of Medicine, 2022).

I've mentioned the concept of quality sleep a few times now, but for many that might be a very abstract concept. When you're unconscious, it's hard to tell what type of sleep you are getting. Or, you might not even realize that there is even a difference in the type of sleep you cycle through in the evening. However, while your eyes are closed and you're checked out into dreamland, a whole host of unique processes are happening in the body to help you recover and prepare for the next day.

There are Two Types of Sleep

The first thing to understand is that there are two main types of sleep: Non-Rapid Eye Movement (NREM) and Rapid Eye Movement (REM). During each of these phases, your body and brain are cycling through extremely specific processes, a key one of which is hormone production.

During NREM, you eventually enter what is called slow-wave sleep (SWS) or deep sleep. **It's at this stage that you secrete human growth hormone (HGH) and start the critical restorative processes such as tissue growth and repair, immune function, and energy restoration.** It's one of the most important parts of the sleep cycle because it's when your body both heals itself and replenishes those extremely important hormones you need for the following day.

If you don't enter deep sleep – either because you go to bed too late and don't have time to get there or you have interrupted sleep that doesn't allow you to cycle through the three stages of NREM and REM that constitute of good night's sleep – **then your body won't have time to restore and produce those hormones.**

As much as we'd love to think that sleep is as easy as closing your eyes and then waking up refreshed, your body has to first cycle through specific phases which constitute a full sleep "cycle."

There are three stages of NREM – stage 1 is light sleep, stage 2 is a deeper stage of light sleep, and stage 3 is deep sleep – and one stage of REM. A typical sleep cycle starts with stage 1, moves into stage 2, followed by stage 3, then drops back into stage 2, before hitting REM.

Each sleep cycle lasts around 90 to 110 minutes and you will experience four or five of these cycles every night. But, if you are up until 2 a.m. staring at your phone and have to be up at 7 a.m. to get ready for work, it's impossible for you to get in those four or five cycles required to create the hormones that your body needs to function effectively the next day. Your cortisol will be imbalanced, so it will be harder to wake up and to fall asleep later that night. You'll also be less likely to handle any stress that comes your way that day in a healthy and measured way because your cortisol will already be too high.

If you had gotten a proper night's rest, you would have replenished the hormones, your cortisol would have naturally helped wake you up at the appropriate hour, and you would be a lot more prepared to deal with daily stress without freaking out or feeling overwhelmed.

Now, the key word there is "proper" and I'm not talking polite. Wake up to go to the bathroom? That's an interrupted sleep cycle. Stay up late scrolling on your phone? That's an interrupted sleep cycle. Toss and turn with hot flashes for hours? That's – you guessed it – an interrupted sleep cycle.

And, what's telling, is according to Gracom, the majority of her patients don't even realize they aren't getting a good night's sleep. As long as they fall asleep and wake up feeling somewhat rested, most people consider that a good night's work. After all, you're unconscious, for the most part, when all of this is happening, so you have no idea what kind of sleep you are getting and if you got enough of it.

Recently, we've seen an uptick in fitness and sleep trackers that will log your sleep cycle and tell you what type of rest you are getting, but outside of those handy gadgets, which definitely have margins of error, it's difficult to know what's happening while you snooze.

Sleep: Nature's Reset Button—Ruined by Your Phone

Sleep Is When Your Body Makes Your Hormones

You might be thinking that it's not really that big of a deal if you're not getting the exact amount and type of sleep that experts recommend. As long as you're not falling asleep in meetings you're fine, right? That's what caffeine is for, after all.

Unfortunately, it's not as easy as downing multiple espresso shots throughout the day and hoping for the best. That's because, as Dr. Dorfman notes, **sleep isn't just about getting enough rest to feel energized.** Because during each stage of your sleep cycle, your body is actively producing the hormones you need to both recharge from the day you just experienced and reboot for the day ahead, and unfortunately **there's no latte that's going to replicate or replace those hormones for you.**

According to Dr. Dorfman, **the two most significant hormones released are HGH and cortisol.** HGH is released during deep sleep, alongside testosterone, to help you recover, rebuild, and regenerate.

As the name so helpfully implies, HGH helps you to grow and develop muscle, while repairing tissue. If you are injured, sick, recovering from a hard workout, or just have any daily wear and tear that needs to be addressed, HGH is going to help your body do that.

As we age, our levels of HGH naturally decline, along with our ability to get that quality sleep, which is a fun little joke that nature plays on us. You need to sleep to produce the hormone that will help you recover, but issues like menopause or prostate problems can keep you up at night and prevent you from getting that reparative HGH, which your body is already making less of anyways. Quite the sadistic sense of humor our biological systems seem to have.

Cortisol, on the other hand, is a 24-hour hormone that is produced in waves, with the peak hitting around 9 a.m. and a low at midnight.

As you are sleeping, specifically in your REM cycle, notes Dr. Dorfman, your adrenal glands will release pulses of cortisol that gradually increase throughout the night, getting stronger as you reach that eventual apex hour of 9 a.m. to coax your body awake. However, if you prolong bedtime, or keep constantly waking up and disrupting your sleep cycle, you throw the whole delicate system out of balance.

If you don't sleep well, chances are you're probably somewhat aware of that fact. It's hard not to notice you wake up every couple of hours for no apparent reason, or you stare at the ceiling when you should be drifting off into dreamland. But understanding the cause of those sleep issues is a little more complicated as there can be many different root causes to why your sleep is jacked up.

For instance, **if you fall into the category of having trouble falling asleep, odds are you have elevated cortisol** and there's no one real cause that can be singled out for that particular issue, notes Gracom. Everything from exercising or eating too close to bedtime, to menopause giving you hot flashes and making it uncomfortable to sleep.

What It Means When You Wake Up at 2 A.M.

On the other hand, **waking up in the middle of the night**, she explains, **is tied to an imbalance in your cortisol production.** If your body wakes you up naturally between the hours of 2 a.m. and 4 a.m., or you can't sleep later than 5 a.m., your cortisol is spiking at an unnatural time, pulling you out of sleep before your body is ready and messing up your natural rhythm for the day.

Now, you can expect to have cortisol peaking before dawn and dipping in the early evening, throwing your schedule off and making it more difficult to get back into that natural cycle for the following day. Have that happen often enough and you run the risk of chronic issues like exhaustion, irritability, weight gain, and brain fog messing up your whole day, notes Gracom.

Have enough of those days back-to-back and you start to feel out of sync with your body, which could lead to bigger health issues down the road. It's why she says sleep is the most important biological function to stay healthy.

"By hook or crook, protect your sleep," says Gracom.

Tips for Getting Better Sleep

And, people have spent billions of dollars a year doing just that (Polaris Market Research, 2025). From sleep medications to devices to mattresses, the global sleep aid market is valued at over $65 billion a year (and growing).

But, despite dropping their hard-earned cash on everything from white-noise machines to temperature-controlled mattresses and melatonin gummies, **more than a third of Americans report getting less than seven hours of sleep per night** (CDC, 2022). That's just those that report it – as Gracom wisely points out, many people who have disturbed sleep don't necessarily recognize it.

Side-eye to all you night owls staying up into the wee hours of the night. Yes, you're included in that disturbed sleep category, even if you're getting more than seven hours because, as we talked about earlier, **you're getting that sleep at the wrong time of night.**

We know that sleep hygiene is crucial to getting a good night's rest. That means making sure your bedroom is a cozy sleep environment that's cool, dark, quiet, and comfortable with no screens to distract you. It also means establishing a consistent bedtime, avoiding caffeine too late in the day, exercising regularly, avoiding heavy meals at night, and not using your bed for other activities like watching TV, working, or reading. Otherwise you run the risk of your brain associating your bed with stressful or engaging activities and it won't naturally quiet down when bedtime rolls around.

What's truly fascinating to note is that while sleep statistics haven't really changed in over two decades – in 2002, the same National Sleep Foundation Sleep in America poll found that 39 percent of Americans reported getting less than seven hours of sleep a night – back then, many people claimed that a better mattress might be the solution to their sleep woes. In fact, 89 percent of the respondents in the study agreed that a better quality mattress provides a better night's sleep.

The Mattress That Revolutionized Sleep

If there's one person who knows something about mattress quality, it's Pat Hopf. The former chairman and CEO for Sleep Number Bed helped take the fledgling company from a tiny start-up to a billion dollar innovator in the mattress category. In the early 1990s, he was a venture capitalist looking to invest in an air mattress company that promised to make his back pain disappear. Skeptical, he met the founder at his base of operations – his garage – to learn more about this supposedly miraculous new bed.

"I was 41 at the time with a bad back that I had injured playing football when I was 17," explains Hopf. "I would still go out and I would play golf, but my back would tighten up the longer I would play and I would have to take an aspirin. I would probably shoot 37 on the front side and 47 on the back side because my back would get worse and worse as I played."

Bob Walker, the founder of Sleep Number, promised his unique chambered air mattress helped people with bad backs, so Hopf decided to purchase a queen size mattress for $750 before deciding whether or not to invest and help grow the company. "At the time, I had to take around 16 aspirin in order to finish a round of golf," he notes. "Three weeks later, I could play 36 holes without any aspirin and walk and carry my clubs. That was all the due diligence I needed to do." He invested in the company, took over as CEO and chairman, and helped take the company public, with a company value reaching highs of $1.5B.

The secret to that success was a mattress full of air. While today we've become accustomed to mattresses made from foam and adjustable, temperature regulated sleep systems, when Hopf was popping 16 aspirins to get through his round of golf, the standard mattress configuration was a coil and spring setup. As he explains, those didn't exactly set the majority of people up for a comfortable night's sleep, leading to countless complaints of chronic pain.

"If you really think about it, with coil and spring, you're sleeping on steel," says Hopf. "It doesn't make any sense to sleep on steel and think 'Oh boy, I'm going to feel great.' At the time, doctors would even say for a bad back to sleep on the hardest surface possible. And that doesn't make any sense because then why wouldn't I just sleep on the floor?"

Sleep Number, he notes, used a German-based pressure point system in their stores to help people measure the pressure points on their entire bodies when lying on a mattress, using a scale of zero to 100, starting them off at 100 and lowering it down until the pressure was reduced on those points. What they found was that the majority of people – depending on their shape, size, and gender – found the most relief from that pressure and pain at around a 30 or 40, which is a relatively soft, not a firm mattress.

This approach to sleep ushered in a new era in how we thought about our unconscious hours – and the amount we were willing to spend on it.

"The average mattress price for a queen-sized bed back then was $750," says Hopf. "Today the average mattress sells for $3,000. The value that people ascribe to sleep has increased significantly. In 1990 people didn't think that much about sleep because there really weren't any good options. You just did what people had always done: You lie down, you get up in the morning and you feel terrible, but that's the way it is."

Now, however, when people talk about sleep, the concept of uncomfortable mattresses or chronic pain no longer tops the list for what's keeping us awake. When was the last time you woke up in your bed and had to snap, crackle, and pop your back because your mattress was a hard block of squeaky steel springs that didn't support you? One has to wonder what would have happened if screens had never entered the picture and we had simply been granted the gift of more comfortable mattresses instead.

Now Smartphone Screens are Sleep's Worst Enemy

Unfortunately, that is not the timeline we live in. Just as we got our mattress game up to snuff, technology entered the picture and our sleep woes continued, albeit with a different culprit. Instead of pain keeping us from getting quality sleep, screens are now the biggest source of sleep interruption.

You've heard it a million times before that screen use before bedtime is detrimental to your sleep hygiene, but just how bad and why might surprise you. Let's take it back to that circadian rhythm your body is naturally attuned to. Have you ever sat outside, soaking up the sun, and felt that sense of contentment and bliss? That's because natural sunlight is physically good for you. You actually need it on a daily basis to regulate your natural circadian rhythm.

Bright light in the morning helps you to naturally wake up, while dim light in the evening helps you to ease into sleep. It's why during the winter, when daylight hours are more scarce, our moods tend to be a bit more down (Seasonal Affective Disorder, anyone?) and summer, when the days are longer, finds us more energized to be outside and active.

Blue Light Increases Your Cortisol, Which Wrecks Your Sleep

Except, we went ahead and managed to mess that up, as humans are prone to do. Because blue light – the light that emanates from your computer, tablet, and phone screens – is a form of artificial light that tricks your body into thinking it's sunlight and, you guessed it, releases cortisol.

As smart and evolved as humans are, we haven't evolved to be smarter than nature, no matter how many Silicon Valley hot shots want to tell you they've unlocked the secret to longevity via a combo of magic mushrooms, testosterone shots, and daily cold plunges.

The body sees that blue light and it confuses our system, throwing it for a loop when it's supposed to be chilling out and winding down.

If you are looking at a screen before bedtime – and that means one to two hours before you are supposed to be heading into bed, not just directly before bed – your conscious brain may know that you are looking at, say Instagram pictures of your best friend's Italian vacation to the Amalfi Coast (so many aperol spritzes and bowls of pasta, so little time), but your body thinks that little glow from the screen is the same thing as the light that comes from the giant blazing star in the sky and acts accordingly, throwing your circadian rhythm into a tailspin and making it difficult to fall asleep. That's because **your body suppresses the secretion of natural melatonin, the hormone that controls your sleep–wake cycle.**

Why Melatonin Won't Fix Your Sleep

If your first reaction to that revelation is to immediately reach for a melatonin supplement, I'm afraid it's sadly not that easy. Melatonin naturally rises about two hours before that natural bedtime, triggered by your circadian rhythm. Basically, your body sees it's dark outside and soon after begins to release melatonin to tell you it's time to go to bed, correlating with a drop in cortisol, which also furthers that sense of sleepiness.

Many people wrongfully think melatonin makes you fall asleep, when in fact melatonin simply signals to your body that it's time to fall asleep – there's a big difference. It won't make you sleepy, it just creates sleep-inducing signals that tell your body, hey, maybe you should think about heading to bed now buddy, ok? Do you really need to watch yet another episode of the *Great British Bake-Off* when your eyes are feeling heavy?

While short term, some melatonin can be beneficial – specifically for those dealing with the symptoms of jet lag – **long-term and consistent use of melatonin has not been proven to have a lasting benefit.** Not to mention that most of the supplements that contain melatonin are either not getting into your system due to the digestive system breaking them down before they have a chance to fully enter the bloodstream or they don't contain beneficial enough levels of melatonin *(or, any melatonin at all – obligatory warning to stop buying your supplements and vitamins from Amazon, where quality control is non-existent and you have no guarantee that what's in the bottle is what's listed on the label).*

Red Light at Night Also Disrupts Sleep

Gracom notes that blue light isn't the only light you need to be wary of before bedtime – as red light becomes more prevalent for at-home usage, specifically in beauty devices like masks, patches, and wands for anti-aging skin-care benefits, many people have a tendency to use them at night. She notes that while **red light** has been shown to have healthy benefits for lowering cortisol during the daytime, **when used before bedtime, it can actually raise your levels of cortisol** (Figueiro and Rea, 2010). Because, once again, your body can't tell the difference between a form of artificial light and that big ball of UV light in the sky. So, by all means, throw on one of those Hannibal Lecter contraptions to promote collagen and keep your skin looking fresh and healthy, but be sure you're doing it in the morning or afternoon and don't do it as part of your nightly skin regimen.

Put Your Phone on "Do Not Disturb" or Better Yet, in Another Room

Artificial light isn't the only issue that screen time before bedtime can have on your sleep quality (or lack thereof). Imagine you're winding down for the night, feeling calm, relaxed, and ready for a great night's rest. Your phone, which, of course, is plugged in next to your bed on the nightstand (because where else would it be) suddenly pings or vibrates. It's a text from your boss. That project you've been working on for months was rejected by the client and the whole office is in disarray. Everyone is panicking because this project was a big part of the budget for the rest of the year. You need to come up with a whole new plan tomorrow or you'll lose the business and everyone is counting on you to lead them.

Or, maybe it's a friend you haven't talked to in a while. They're mad at you because you haven't been around and you haven't reached out to see how they were. You get into a huge argument that results in some pretty mean things being said back and forth, and now a group text is blowing up with other friends getting involved and asking what the heck is going on. Three messages turns into 30 messages and now someone is posting nasty things on social media at midnight. Sweet dreams?

In theory, keeping our phones near our beds makes perfect sense. Part of our brains can rationalize the whole, "what if there is an emergency and someone needs to get in touch with me?" line of thinking.

Considering 75 percent of Americans live in a home without a landline, that's not an unreasonable train of thought (Blumberg, Luke and NCHS, 2024). For the majority of us, our cell phone is our only method of communication, so we've been trained to respond to every little ping, ding, and buzz as if it's an urgent communiqué because we have no way to know the difference between a buzz that signifies a text from a friend with urgent news and a buzz that tells us a brand we follow posted a new video on Instagram.

Once again, evolution can't tell the difference either, so **when we pick up that phone and look at those push notifications and texts and emails, our cortisol spikes. And, when that happens at bedtime, you can guess what happens next.** Hello, pre-dawn wake up and all the lovely side effects that come with an inadequate night's sleep for the next day.

Plus, if you bring those gadgets and devices to bed, you've got the double-edged sword of being tempted to scroll through all those apps and videos and streaming services that are available at your fingertips. They don't call it mindless scrolling for nothing – one minute you've picked up the phone to glance briefly at whatever caused it to buzz, the next it's three hours later and you've been staring at Instagram videos and aren't quite sure how you got to your cousin's best friend's art teacher throwing paint-covered croissants at a wall while yelling about the French Revolution.

Is it entertaining? Mildly. Is it worth the bad day you're going to have tomorrow? Absolutely not.

Train Your Brain Your Bed Is for Sleep and Sex Only

Even worse are those that use their bed as a multifunctional space. Dragging your computer into the bed to work late because you think it's a better idea than sitting at your desk until the wee hours? I promise you that it's actually a worse idea – your bed should be reserved for sleep and extracurricular activities of the intimate variety. Anything else and you are training your brain to associate it with stressful or invigorating (no, not the good kind of invigorating) activities and that will cause – you guessed it – cortisol to spike.

I'm guessing you don't get very sleepy at your desk that often and that's because you don't regularly sleep at your desk. It's not a place you associate with sleep and calmness. The bedroom should always be a sanctuary and a respite to help keep your association with that space calming and relaxing. As Gracom says, **protect your sleep, and sometimes that means protect it from your worst impulses, meaning ditch the devices.**

There are some instances where even when you follow good sleep hygiene, you still struggle to get a proper night's rest. This is a particular problem with aging, specifically with women as they hit menopause, and many men (andropause or manopause, if you will). We'll dive more in depth into the specifics of these issues in the next chapter, but for those experiencing this stage, one of the main symptoms of hormones declining are hot flashes, which can make it difficult to fall asleep, or wake you up in the middle of the night drenched in sweat.

For others, despite their best efforts to block out stress and keep cortisol balanced, they find it just too difficult to stay level in a tech-focused world.

Now There's an Easy Way to Regulate Your Cortisol for Great Sleep

One of the main benefits of our Rebalance system is helping to regulate cortisol throughout the day, ensuring that it follows a natural flow cycle, helping you to get a proper night's rest and get your body back into its optimal rhythm.

Our clinical testing on our lozenge systems, taken three times a day, using proven herbs and botanicals, demonstrates it could have a positive impact on the daily lives of men and women who just want to get a good night's sleep and feel more like themselves.

And our due diligence, as Pat Hopf would say, is the number of customers who tell us their sleep has been improved because of our products, especially menopausal women struggling with night sweats and hot flashes. They rejoice that they feel healthier, their brain fog has vanished, and they have mental clarity and energy they lacked when their sleep was impaired.

Why the Usual Sleep Aids Create More Problems Than They Solve

Traditional sleep aids are a temporary solution that don't get to the root cause of sleep disturbances – stress and a disruption to your circadian rhythm due to the demands of an increasingly more online world.

Pharmaceuticals, alcohol, drugs, and melatonin are short-term, problematic Band-Aids that lead to bigger problems down the road or are mis-guided aids.

While melatonin is a fabulous ingredient to help trigger a chain of events to help you fall asleep, the supplement is eliminated from your system within a few hours of supplementation. Which means, yup, you guessed it, you're wide awake at 2 a.m.

Sure, you can take an Ambien and fall asleep right away, but not only do studies show that it knocks you out and forgoes the body's ability to enter into a natural circadian rhythm completely – in other words, you don't make the hormones you need to function the next day, often waking up exhausted because regeneration didn't occur – you can also wake up in your kitchen making a ham and Snickers sandwich wearing a suit coat with no pants, opera music blaring at full volume and every light on in your house with absolutely no idea how you got there or why any of the things in front of you are currently happening. That's mildly concerning, to say the least.

Sleep is important, but not doing random, unexplainable activities while drugged out on a pharmaceutical is also pretty important, too (Figure 2.1).

Sleep health takes a full day

- Get natural morning light
- Take a daily walk outdoors
- Avoid stimulants late in the day
- Limit screen time before bed
- Create a wind-down routine
- Keep a consistent sleep schedule

Figure 2.1 Do You Have Good Sleep Hygiene? *Source:* Rebalance Health

Chapter 3

Hot Flashes, Mood Swings & Midlife Mayhem? Blame Cortisol, Not Just Estrogen

Drenched in sweat, your every nerve tingling and your body on fire, you rip off the last shred of your clothing and throw it on the bedroom floor, waiting for a release. Instead, the pressure keeps building as you writhe in bed and dawn's early light begins to peek through the curtains.

The clock ticks by, uncaring that you are enduring a slow form of torture as your body thrashes on the bed. Unsure you can take it anymore, you moan loudly, not caring who hears you, gripping the bed as the heat intensifies.

Every nerve of your body is on fire and even your normally soft and cozy bed sheets feel like sandpaper as they slide across your skin. You kick those off, too, but still can't find relief from the unending waves of heat rolling across your body. Every sensation is too much – you're a pressure cooker just waiting to explode.

You let out another frustrated moan as you slam your hands into the pillow, prompting your partner to crack open their eyes from their place beside you in bed. "Hot flashes again?" they ask groggily. You nod in frustration, trying not to go into a full meno-rage as they drift back off into the peaceful sleep that eludes you, tossing and turning as you try to find a cool space that does not exist on the mattress.

How is it that hours before you were exhausted and barely able to keep your eyes open, but now, when you should be blissfully asleep, you are instead wide awake, uncomfortable, sweating, and simmering in anger at your partner simply because they're not feeling like they just descended into the ninth level of hell to take a Jacuzzi soak in a lava pit?

For something with such a benign moniker, hot flashes – and menopause as a whole – disrupt so much of your core operating systems, with sleep being the one that is largely dismissed as just another thing women need to deal with.

It was only recently, however, that the topic of menopause even entered the mainstream conversation. Women knew that it was something that was in their future – some closer than others – but the absolute havoc that it wreaks and any possible solutions to mitigate those symptoms weren't discussed in casual conversation. A knowing glance between women as hot flashes hit, perhaps, but all too often there was an expectation of suffering in silence.

Our society has always been prudish at its best and negligent at its worst around the topic of women's health, meaning so-called "women's issues" were impolite to speak of up until quite recently.

We've seen erectile dysfunction ads on television since the late 1990s, yet the very first Super Bowl commercial mentioning menopause didn't happen until 2023, almost 30 years later.

Men, who aren't usually known for candidly talking about their health problems, have had more information about a so-called taboo health topic broadcast to them since 1998, but women, who are going through a major and completely natural health and life change that they often want to talk to each other about and share information on, are only just now being armed with the information they need to be prepared for this important new phase.

Not wanting the cycle to repeat, older generations are making it their mission to speak up and educate younger generations with candid talk of what is happening to their bodies so that the next generation isn't faced with the same bewildering feelings when perimenopause hits, convinced they are going crazy when their estrogen decides to take a hike and the mere sound of their partner breathing is enough to throw them into an epic rage – or too scared to talk about how debilitating their hot flashes are because they are worried about ageism in the workplace, or confused about what is even happening to their body because their doctor keeps telling them they are too young to start showing symptoms.

Why Your Doctor Isn't Much Help

That confusion women feel, for the most part, has not been alleviated by their healthcare providers. In a 2018 AARP survey of more than 400 women aged 50 to 59, 42 percent of women never even discussed menopause with a healthcare provider and only one in five of those women were even referred to a menopause specialist (Wolff, 2018).

Part of that may be because doctors aren't trained in menopause and how to manage it or mitigate the symptoms. A 2019 Mayo Clinic study of 183 medical residents found that while around 94 percent believed that it was important or very important to be trained to manage menopause, only about 7 percent felt that they were adequately prepared to do so (Kling et al., 2019).

Add on to that the fact that there's no such thing as a "typical" menopause – some women start perimenopause as early as their 30s while others might not start until their mid-50s – and you have medical professionals who are woefully unprepared to help guide women through this monumental shift in their lives.

As Dr. Dorfman points out, much of that can be attributed to the fact that science, up until very recently, has largely failed to actually study women's health in any real detail, meaning they are unable to train doctors on how to advise their patients.

"For much of medical history, women's health issues, including menopause, were not a priority in research and medical education, contributing to a lack of medical resources and knowledge about menopause," says Dr. Dorfman. "Gender bias still exists in medicine and it's not only in menopause. Separate out white males and then take everyone else and you can honestly say there's not enough medical research, whether it's heart disease or dementia."

In fact, it wasn't until 1993 that Congress passed a law that women and people of color must be included in medical research studies (Mastroianni, Faden and Federman, 1994). Up until that point, scientists and doctors could conduct a study on women's reproductive health and legally not include any women in the study. Which makes no logical sense, but up until that point was the norm for clinical research.

And, it certainly explains why erectile dysfunction ads have been running seemingly non-stop since Y2K and we're only now starting to really see any in-depth attention being paid to women's health – once you start including women in studies, you start to realize they have unique physiological needs and issues that need to be addressed. A huge shock to literally no woman reading this.

Science isn't the only one responsible for this mass misunderstanding around menopause, however. It's a complicated net of factors that encompasses everything from ageism to representation in the media, notes Dr. Dorfman.

Look at depictions of women experiencing menopause in TV and movies and oftentimes you'll see it played for laughs, as something to be mocked or made light of. The stereotypical hormonal woman acting irrational as she fans herself and starts shedding clothing, erupting at her poor, suffering husband and oblivious children.

And, while many women can and do find the humor (sometimes laughing is the only way to keep from crying), there's a difference when you are the butt of the joke instead of humor being used as a coping mechanism or a way to feel acknowledged and seen in the cultural dialogue.

The reality for anyone experiencing menopause is that it's a truly complicated time in a woman's life when their body feels foreign to them and it feels like society and sometimes even their own family wants them to just not make a big deal about it because really, how bad could it be? It's just some hot flashes and mood swings, right?

But, it's that attitude of sweeping menopause under the proverbial rug – plus the overall marginalization of women over 40 in Western culture – that makes this such a difficult transition. Add to the fact that for centuries it's been a topic that's felt almost shameful to talk about due to our almost Puritan attitudes toward women's reproductive health, and you have many women in the throes of menopause who don't even realize that some of the symptoms they are experiencing are even part of this natural life stage.

Menopause Is More Than Hot Flashes

While mostly everyone knows about hot flashes, issues like mood swings, weight gain, low libido, brain fog, and low energy aren't often talked about in context with the changes that happen to the body during this stage. It can almost be a relief to learn that the reason you went DEFCON 1 on your partner over a single dirty dish left overnight in the sink was not, in fact, because you are experiencing a Jekyll and Hyde personality disorder, but rather a typical emotional fluctuation from your hormones exiting stage left. There is, in fact, a completely valid medical reason that you feel like a totally different person and you are not, in fact, losing your mind, even though it kind of feels like it in the moment.

Thankfully, the last few years has seen a shift in the conversation around menopause, which has led to more openness about the topic. Celebrities like Naomi Watts and Courteney Cox have talked openly about the symptoms of menopause and lent their image and star power to ads that raise awareness about what to expect and what is happening to your body during this life stage.

While there's no version of *The Care and Keeping of You* for menopausal women (although I'd argue that hopefully this chapter can be something close to it), the fact that we've gotten to a place where we're even saying the word "menopause" on TV and not using hot flash as a euphemism for everything that happens to the body during menopause shows we've advanced our thinking and that's thanks to a host of dedicated women who have advocated to raise awareness for women's health and change the way we think about aging.

We're no longer obsessed with this idea of being forever young, but rather we've embraced a new way of thinking about age that's more centered around living longer, healthier lives and the quality of those lives rather than trying to stop the aging process altogether.

The most important message that more menopausal women need to fully realize is that there is absolutely nothing wrong with them. Menopause is a natural stage of life for women. While symptoms, severity, and the age it starts might differ, menopause is, say it with me now, normal. You are normal. You may feel anything but right now, but you are absolutely not alone in this feeling – every woman who enters into menopause experiences it her own way, and almost all women feel like they've become a completely different person because of how dramatic the effects of a drop in hormone levels can be.

The first step to normalizing anything is understanding it. You might be thinking that it's your body and you know the ins and outs of it better than anyone. Fair point. But, one thing we heard over and over again from women when we were testing the Rebalance system was how menopause made them feel like strangers in their own bodies.

The changes that happen coupled with the lack of answers from doctors leaves many women adrift and alienated as they both see and feel shifts in how their body looks and reacts. Many describe it as a jarring change that happens swiftly and leaves them not feeling like themselves physically, mentally, and emotionally.

Your friends and family will definitely notice – if they're brave, they'll have a comment about your sudden mood swings, but the majority will walk on eggshells for fear of setting off an emotional eruption at Mount Menopause. So, while absolutely normal, it's definitely not a fun experience for anyone, and not something you need to suffer through without anything to alleviate your symptoms.

The Rebalance Hot Flash System for Better Sleep and Fewer Hot Flashes

When we first began testing for the Rebalance system, we started hearing interesting feedback from women who were also going through menopause at the time. Many claimed that they were seeing a significant decrease in the frequency and severity of their hot flashes.

Since our initial goal was focused on cortisol and sleep, we were pleasantly surprised with these anecdotes, but thought they had to be outliers. Gradually, we heard more stories from women who were seeing their symptoms decline – fewer hot flashes, increased mental clarity, improved quality of sleep, enhanced mood and libido, quicker recovery from working out, and improved skin and nails.

We realized that we had not only created a unique system to help support cortisol production in the body, we'd also created an alternative treatment option for menopause symptoms.

But we had to be sure as we knew a drug-free, hormone-free solution to hot flashes would be life changing for so many.

So **we commissioned what's called an institutional review board open label study,** led by Dr. Dorfman. The study consisted of 104 women with a mean age of 53 who had not taken hormone replacement therapy (HRT) in the past 12 months and were all experiencing debilitating hot flashes and other menopausal symptoms.

Each was given a 90-day supply of our Hot Flash System, which consists of three different lozenges a day, and were asked to provide feedback via a daily questionnaire. They also underwent four separate blood draws, taken at the start of the study and every 30 days after, to measure hormone levels and other menopausal parameters.

The results were mind blowing and that's not an exaggeration. An astounding 100 percent of participants reported a reduction in menopausal symptoms, while 80 percent saw a significant reduction in hot flashes, and 25 percent of participants reported that their hot flashes were completely eliminated while taking the Hot Flash System.

For anyone who has ever experienced a hot flash, you know that any sort of reduction in hot flashes can feel monumental. The fact that **80 percent of those women saw a significant reduction** was one of the most incredible statistics we saw throughout our entire testing – so much so that the North American Menopause Society took note and published our preliminary data in their journal *Menopause* in 2023.

Men Also Have a Change Called Andropause

Men also experience their own form of menopause, referred to as andropause. It's not quite the same shock to the system as menopause, occurring gradually over time as men age, and is typified by a decline in levels of certain hormones – most notably testosterone – with symptoms developing slowly over time.

"Starting in the mid-30s and ending roughly in their 70s, men experience a steady, gradual decrease in their hormone levels," says Dr. Dorfman.

But, surprisingly, some of the symptoms they experience mirror those that women do.

Dr. Dorfman told me that about 80 percent of his male patients over the age of 40 come into his office complaining of feeling hot in bed. Sound familiar? That's because those men are experiencing a hot flash. So men are experiencing some of the exact same symptoms as women, just at one-tenth of the severity.

Plus, women's hormone decrease happens as an intense drop during a much more condensed period of time – 7–14 years on average – almost as if the rug is pulled out from under them all at once, so everything feels very sudden. It also doesn't help that typically, women tend to be much more in tune with their bodies and their emotions, not to mention have a far more sensitive nervous system, so symptoms will hit them much more intensely.

Which, as any woman who has suddenly burst into tears over a toilet paper commercial can attest, that emotional whiplash is intense and can make you feel like your emotions are having a royal rumble and battling each other for control of your brain at any given moment.

Understanding Menopause and Treatment Options

For centuries, women in menopause have had few options to control their menopause symptoms. Now, marketers have seen a golden opportunity as the taboo gradually lifts. In the United States alone, 6,000 women enter menopause every day, giving many an opportunistic individual the ability to present products to a population that grows more and more desperate for solutions to solve their symptoms and feel like themselves again (Society for Women's Health Research, 2025).

As fun as drenching your shirt right before a big presentation at work because of yet another hot flash can be, or irrationally freaking out because you've just realized your teenager is the loudest chewer you've ever encountered in the history of humans, it's a lot nicer to not have to carry extra clothing around in your purse or lash out at your loved ones over things that never used to send you into spirals of rage before.

The last few decades has seen a rise in HRT, but there are some risks with that treatment option, and, as Dr. Dorfman points out, it's not a treatment option that should be chosen as the first choice for your symptoms without first exploring alternatives.

Before you can understand how to manage your menopause symptoms, you first need to understand what is happening during this phase. While women are generally well prepared for what happens during puberty and their childbearing years, menopause often remains a mystery – to them and to many doctors.

So I asked Dr. Dorfman, a leader in the topic of hormonal health, to share his insights for this chapter to help demystify menopause as a form of continuing education and preparation. Whether you are currently in the throes of it or want to be prepared for what's to come – or support those in your life who will be dealing with it – this chapter will explain what menopause is, the symptoms you may experience, and the treatment options that are available and their pros and cons.

How Women's Bodies Change During Menopause

In the simplest of terms, menopause marks the end of a woman's reproductive years. It often occurs during the ages of 45 and 55 (but can happen earlier for some) and consists of three phases: perimenopause, menopause, and post-menopause.

Perimenopause is the 4- to 10-year period when symptoms typically begin to appear, while menopause is marked by the end of a 12-month phase when a woman has not had a period.

Post-menopause, aptly, is the time after menopause, and while some post-menopausal women will no longer experience symptoms, many still continue to exhibit them for months or even years after they have moved out of the menopausal stage.

In the sage words of Al Pacino in *The Godfather: Part III*, "just when you thought you were out, they pull you back in." Because your hormones are a little bit gangster like that – you might think you've escaped the worst of it, but then they seem to scheme and plot and you're left raging nonsensically in the kitchen over your pasta and chianti

But many women can experience menopause at an earlier age and an even more expedited timeline through what's often referred to as medical menopause. This happens when a woman's ovaries are surgically removed, usually for medical conditions like endometriosis, uterine fibroids, ovarian cysts, or reducing the risk of ovarian cancer. Women who are undergoing treatment for ovarian or breast cancer will oftentimes find that the chemotherapy drugs or pelvic radiation therapy can induce menopause, another form of medical menopause (DePolo, 2025).

The hormones that are typically being referred to when doctors talk about menopause are estrogen and progesterone; however testosterone is also affected during menopause as Dr. Dorfman notes that all three see significant decline.

Estrogen plays a role in reproductive health for women. It's a chemical messenger hormone that tells your body when to start or stop certain sexual and reproductive health processes. It is also present in men, but at much lower levels.

During puberty, estrogen levels rise and lead to changes in the body, like breasts and more curvaceous features. As part of the menstrual cycle, estrogen helps keep your period regular, playing a role in ovulation and thickening the lining of your uterus to prepare it for pregnancy. Estrogen will hit its peak during ovulation – when the ovaries release an egg – and help thin the cervical mucus to help make it easier for sperm to fertilize the recently released egg.

Estrogen is also the hormone that makes intercourse more comfortable, lubricating the vaginal walls and ensuring penetrative sex is enjoyable and not painful. It's like the get-it-on hormone, doing everything it can to help the reproductive process. Meaning when it falls off that menopausal cliff, suddenly sex becomes a lot less pleasant. Which is difficult to explain to your partner when they're sexed up and ready for action and your intimate regions are feeling drier than the Atacama Desert. Not really a "take me now, oh baby, oh baby" vibe.

Progesterone's main function is to help prepare the lining of the uterus for a fertilized egg to implant and, subsequently, grow. If the egg is fertilized, progesterone will increase and the uterine lining will thicken. Progesterone levels will continue to increase throughout your pregnancy, providing nutrients for the embryo, culminating in the highest levels of progesterone production in your third trimester.

That high progesterone is what prevents your from ovulating and helps you avoid preterm labor. It's also what helps prepare your breasts for breastfeeding. If the egg is not fertilized, progesterone will decrease and the uterine lining will break down, triggering the start of your menstrual cycle. Progesterone will decrease as your body prepares itself for menopause, as part of the end of your ovulation and reproductive years.

Just as those men have low levels of estrogen and progesterone in their bodies, so, too do women have low levels of testosterone in their bodies, produced by the ovaries. While the majority of the testosterone produced by women is converted into the female hormone estradiol – a form of estrogen – the small amounts that remain are responsible for libido in women.

Many women find in the years leading up to menopause that they are in their sexual prime and have more interest in sex and more desire than in previous years. Scientists have hypothesized that age 35 is when a woman hits her peak for sexual desire, as that is her body's way of telling her that her naturally fertile years are soon coming to a close (Wieczorek et al., 2022).

Obviously, women are having children later in life these days thanks to advancements in science and better maternal care, but, like with technology, our bodies haven't evolved with changing norms in society. It might be more common to have children later in life, but no one told biology that, so those hormones are still sending signals that it's time to get busy.

But, **when testosterone levels begin their downward trend in women during menopause, it has a direct impact on their libido.** Coupled with the loss of estrogen making the sex they are having feel painful, it's no surprise that many menopausal women report a significant shift in their sex lives once perimenopause starts.

Men also experience their own issues with sexual performance as they age; however, thanks to those little blue pills that have been all over our television screens for the past few decades, they've been able to navigate around that particular issue without too many hurdles. Meaning in many heterosexual couples, you have one partner who is perpetually exhausted, emotional, and not the least bit interested in sexy time and you have the other partner who is ready to go whenever and wherever thanks to his new pharmaceutical special helper. **The disconnect has led to a rise in intimacy issues between couples, especially around intercourse.**

How Menopause Affects Your Sex Life

We conducted a general population study of 1,000 menopausal women between the ages of 40–55, all in long-term relationships. Fifty-five percent of those women were perimenopausal and experiencing symptoms, 30 percent were currently going through menopause, and 16 percent had recently completed menopause.

Of those respondents, 75 percent said sex was the furthest thing from their mind when experiencing menopause symptoms, while 64 percent said they would have a lot more sex if their menopause symptoms would go away. The biggest hurdles for impacting their sex lives included fatigue (74 percent), mood changes (69 percent), trouble sleeping (67 percent), and hot flashes (67 percent).

Of the women surveyed, 58 percent said that they regularly engaged in sexual activity (weekly or more frequently) before menopause, but that number dropped to just 34 percent after menopause symptoms started. Yet only 42 percent of these women discussed the impact that menopause was having on their sex lives with their spouse or partner. And only 24 percent discussed the impact that menopause had on their sex lives with their doctor, with 60 percent receiving no information, treatment, or support.

I don't know about you, but those results were shocking to me. Intimacy is a foundation of healthy relationships, and when menopause has such a profound impact on your sex life, that's something you should be able to discuss with your partner and feel like you can go to your doctor for resources to help support you. Instead, many women are accepting this seismic sexual shift as just another fact of life and allowing it to impact their relationships and their physical and emotional health.

Dr. Dorfman notes that vaginal dryness is a common symptom of menopause, while a decrease in sexual desire and satisfaction is also normal. Yet many women, as we found out with our intimacy study, don't talk about their sexual dissatisfaction with their doctors or their partners. No one expects you to feel like a horny teenager all the time; however, that doesn't mean you should hit menopause and just expect to be celibate, either. There can be a balance between the two, but **the first step is to recognize that this decrease in sexual desire and painful intercourse caused by vaginal dryness are both extremely normal symptoms associated with menopause.**

Your hormones have a direct impact on arousal, but menopause doesn't mean you have to just accept that these symptoms are going to fundamentally change your dynamic with your partner and your own sexual satisfaction. It takes two to tango, after all, so talk to your partner about how you are feeling and what is happening and don't feel like these symptoms are something that you can't speak to your doctor about – removing the stigma is the first step to finding a solution.

Depending on how good (or bad) your sex education was in high school, this could all be information you already know about your hormones and your cycle. But, menopause barely gets a mention in most sex education curriculum. Granted, most 16-year-olds aren't too concerned about what's happening next month, let alone what's happening to them or a potential partner or loved one

40 years from now; however, does that mean we shouldn't be educating teenagers about their bodies?

It goes back to one of the largest problems with menopause in that no one talks about it until it's actually happening. With that in mind, let's have our own mini-version of adult sex education – no boring textbooks or pop quizzes or awkward demonstrations involving prophylactics and fruit, promise – and explain what to expect when menopause begins.

Why Menopause Is Unpredictable

The first lesson is that there truly is no such thing as a typical menopause experience. Menopause symptoms are unique to each woman, from the severity to the combination. There's no way to predict how you will be affected. Many women don't even realize the symptoms they are experiencing are from menopause – but you might have been wondering why you were constantly exhausted, overheated, and ready to snap at everyone in your vicinity if they so much as twitched a muscle wrong.

The most common and easily recognizable symptoms are vasomotor symptoms, more widely known as hot flashes and night sweats. Hot flashes are wavelike sensations of intense heat that come on suddenly, usually starting in the neck area and radiating through the face and body. They will cause you to perspire heavily, which can lead to clothing stains and discomfort – issues that can cause embarrassment when you are out in public or major inconveniences for those women who are still in an office or public-facing setting. Not to mention the annoyance of ruining shirt after shirt with sweat stains from something that can't be controlled or predicted.

Night sweats are simply hot flashes that happen at night, and they often leave you drenched in a puddle of sweat, disrupting your sleep while you wait for the flash to pass, then get out of bed to change your clothes and possibly even the sheets if you can't find a dry patch to settle in to.

How Menopause Affects Sleep

Being woken up in the middle of your sleep cycle is already bad enough, but if you then are kept even more awake trying to change your clothes and bedding, **the chances of you getting enough of that precious deep sleep to make the necessary cortisol for the day are extremely slim,** leaving you deficient for the day ahead. It's a near nightly cycle for women who deal with the symptom, putting them at an increased risk for having elevated cortisol levels, which, as we discussed in Chapter 2, affects everything from your immune system to your metabolism to your mood.

Speaking of sleep, menopause can directly contribute to sleep disturbances. In addition to the aforementioned night sweats, which play a big role in impacting your nightly rest, those **lower levels of estrogen and progesterone are also responsible for insomnia and frequent awakenings.** Estrogen influences serotonin (a.k.a. the happy hormone), a neurotransmitter that regulates sleep. Progesterone has a calming effect and promotes sleep. **Lower levels of both will naturally disturb your regular sleep cycle,** meaning – you guessed it – no deep sleep and an increased potential for skyrocketing cortisol.

In what will come as a great shock to no one, many menopausal women report a lack of energy during this phase. Obviously, all the interrupted sleep and increase in insomnia might have something to do with that. However, your hormones are also plotting against you there, as well. **Those reduced estrogen, progesterone, and testosterone levels can all lead to a general decline in energy levels,** says Dr. Dorfman, plus testosterone is an essential hormone for muscle health and general vitality. Without that energy to get up and go, your regularly scheduled program of activities can seem insurmountable – mustering the energy to work out or cook a healthy meal might become more of a chore, and even your usual social activities may fall by the wayside as you find yourself more tired and less motivated to leave the comfort of your cozy couch and comfort food.

Menopause and Weight Gain

While many women expect to gain weight with age, most attribute it to middle age and don't think too much more about it. Age is a contributing factor, but Dr. Dorfman says it is in fact your hormones to blame for the extra weight you might be carrying around, especially in the midsection.

"**Estrogen helps regulate fat distribution, and its decline can lead to increased visceral fat** [the hidden fat that wraps around your abdominal organs], which is associated with metabolic disorders," says Dr. Dorfman. So, instead of your weight being evenly distributed around the body, that decrease in estrogen means that it begins to accumulate in the abdominal area and becomes harder to lose, despite doing the same healthy eating habits and exercise you've always done.

Dr. Dorfman points out that **menopause also has the potential to affect your thyroid hormones, which can impact your metabolism.** If your metabolism slows down, you won't burn as many calories as you usually do, which will contribute to that weight gain. And, if all of that wasn't enough, **spiking cortisol levels from your lack of sleep are directly tied to, you guessed it, an increase in abdominal fat.**

It's a triple threat that means you have to work three times as hard to maintain your typical fitness level. Not that women aren't used to working harder than everyone else to achieve the same outcome, but it's kind of insulting when your own body starts taking cues from the patriarchy.

Why You Have Mood Swings

For anyone who thought they'd escaped the mini-hell of PMS mood swings because their periods were stopping with menopause, Dr. Dorfman has some bad news for you: "Fluctuating and decreased hormone levels can contribute to mood swings, anxiety, depression, and cognitive issues like memory lapses and difficulty concentrating," he explains. "Estrogen has a neuroprotective effect and influences neurotransmitter activity. Estrogen and progesterone influence neurotransmitter systems like serotonin and GABA, which are critical for maintaining energy and mood."

While an impact on mood could mean different things for different people, common complaints for menopausal women include everything from irritability to anxiety to depression, oftentimes in women who have no history of mental health issues. This explains why your family is under the impression that you've been kidnapped and switched with an angry velociraptor that they need to be very cautious approaching and under no circumstances make any sudden movements around.

Menopause and Bone Health

Finally, if all of that wasn't enough to deal with, **estrogen plays an absolutely crucial role in maintaining bone density.** Once it begins its decline, there is an increased potential for acceleration of bone loss, so **women experiencing menopause are more at risk for osteoporosis and fractures.** Because you didn't have enough stressing you out, now you get to add easily broken bones to the list.

Solutions Are Available

Hearing the potential symptoms that await – or recognizing what you're currently going through and understanding that they may be tied to your menopause – can feel very doom and gloom. But, I don't want this to feel discouraging. Understanding and being able to identify where these symptoms are coming from is the first step in helping you work toward removing that feeling of helplessness and working toward a solution. Because there are solutions available.

However, here, too, there needs to be more education. The pharmaceutical industry is not known for being altruistic, and, while the newfound empowerment that has come from discussing menopause more openly, it has also brought with it some bad actors looking to take advantage of an untapped market desperate for relief. Nowhere has this been more evident than in the field of HRT.

Hormone Replacement Therapy Isn't One Size Fits All

Hormone replacement therapy has an extremely complicated legacy. It was first prescribed in the United Kingdom in the 1960s, but it didn't make its way into the United States for menopause treatment until clinical trials began in 1993. **HRT consists of supplementing the declining levels of hormones with creams, pills, pellets, gels, patches, or injections to create the right balance that lessens the severity of the fluctuations of estrogen, progesterone, and testosterone.** As Dr. Dorfman notes, it requires closely monitoring the blood levels of each patient in order to determine the right mix and levels of hormones to supplement. That's because there's no one-size-fits-all fix for menopause because not everyone's hormone levels will fluctuate at the same levels.

In the early days of HRT, there were some alarming studies – specifically the infamous Women's Health Initiative (WHI) trial and the UK Million Women Study – that showed women using HRT were at an increased risk of blood clots, stroke, breast cancer, and ovarian cancer (The Conversation, 2015). At the time, it was found that women in menopause taking a combination of estrogen and progestin (a synthetic form of progesterone) were at a higher risk of developing breast cancer or stroke.

Now, there were many issues with the WHI study in particular, most notably that the HRT being given to women contained over 20 different forms of synthetic estrogen and progesterone that came from horses. Yes, you read that right. Humans only make three types of estrogen, so the decision to give women 20 different forms of estrogen and progesterone and to source the remaining forms from horses was an interesting one, to put it generously.

In 2002, after the publication by the WHI of their findings, doctors dramatically curbed their prescriptions of HRT, and, shortly following that, breast cancer rates soon fell worldwide. Scientists believe that drop in HRT prescriptions helped avoid tens of thousands of cases of breast cancer during that time period. We now know that this study was deeply flawed, as was the HRT that was being given to the women at the time, but the damage had been done.

While some doctors are still hesitant to recommend HRT, recently, we've seen an uptick in HRT as a viable treatment option for menopause symptoms. What changed? Doctors figured out what they got wrong the first time around, specifically giving horse hormones to women. Go figure.

Today, doctors use a bioidentical form of micronized progesterone that is more similar to that naturally produced by women's ovaries and has fewer side effects. Also, not from a horse, so we're already doing way better than we were in the 1990s, but that was a low bar. Doctors also will use much lower doses for HRT than they had in the past, in addition to starting women on therapy at a younger age (between ages 50 and 60, rather than over 60) when it is safest to start HRT.

But, that doesn't mean HRT is not without risks, and doctors have gone from being reluctant to prescribe it to much too eager to put their menopausal patients on HRT as a first option, rather than exploring alternatives first. Because HRT is not necessarily the right choice for everyone. There is no magic number for your hormone levels that everyone needs to be at.

People assume that more is better, but everyone's optimum levels are different. Take men and testosterone, for example. "I've had 70-year-old men come in with total testosterone levels of 900 – they don't have any symptoms of anything," says Dr. Dorfman. "They have normal libido and sexual function, they go to the gym, they're not overweight, and everything's great. Then I have men come in with testosterone levels of like 500 and they are exactly the same. In other words, 500 is perfect for them. They don't need to be 900 because at 500 they function perfectly normally – they are healthy, they look good. So, I think conceptually, people are just making the assumption that more testosterone is better. You have to treat the patient, not the labs."

The main issue with HRT today is that it's a cash business for many doctors, something I liken to Botox. Is there any reason a dentist should be injecting someone's wrinkles with Botox? Absolutely not – they know much less about the anatomy of the face and aren't trained in the same rigorous way as dermatologists and plastic surgeons on how to use neuromodulators to smooth and sculpt. TMJ, sure, a dentist is qualified to inject, but for fine lines and wrinkles that makes zero sense.

Yet there are doctors who are not fully trained and appropriately educated on menopause symptoms and hormones who are prescribing HRT to desperate women looking for relief from their symptoms.

Because when you're not sleeping, sweating through multiple shirts a day, and feel like the living embodiment of the red monster face emoji whenever you are minorly inconvenienced, you start to feel pretty desperate for any type of solution.

But, unlike Botox, which, if done incorrectly, will leave you with a frozen face or droopy eyes for a few months and then revert back to your usual face, messing with your hormones can have serious consequences for your health. If a doctor isn't measuring your blood levels to see what it is you are in need of and just throwing a birth control pill at you, you may end up with too much of a hormone your body has a sufficient amount of.

"You can go into any primary care doctor or OB/Gyn and tell them you are having menopause symptoms, but all they are going to do is throw you on hormone therapy," says Dr. Dorfman. "The birth control pill is cheap, it's covered by insurance. They never measure blood levels. They have no idea where you're at and where you're not. It's one-size-fits-all."

While HRT has its place in menopause treatment, it shouldn't be the first treatment option and it should never be a treatment option done without checking where a patient's blood levels are at first. As Dr. Dorfman says, you need to treat the symptoms, not just the labs.

A woman with hot flashes and night sweats is typically dealing with low estrogen, while a woman with mood swings and irritability can attribute that to low estrogen and progesterone. Low libido, decreased strength, and higher percent body fat can be traced back to low testosterone. Dr. Dorfman uses bioidentical creams as topicals pose less of a blot clot risk than ingestibles like the birth control pill. And he notes that if a patient still has her uterus (i.e., they are not a hysterectomy patient), a doctor must always prescribe progesterone, as estrogen on its own in women with a uterus can have an increased risk of endometrial cancer.

HRT Can Only Replace Hormones, Not Fix a Broken Hormone System

In a country where not everyone has the financial means to see a specialist and get customized, specialized care like the type that Dr. Dorfman provides to his patients with hormonal imbalances, most – doctors and patients alike – are doing the best they can with the knowledge and resources they have to help menopausal women in sheer misery find relief. But, that's not good enough.

Women deserve to have the time and attention needed to help them know what is going on with their bodies as an individual, not as a collective. Because there are long-term repercussions to being on HRT. When I hear commercials advertising testosterone shots for young men who have "lost their edge" I can't help but shake my head. **What no one explains to these patients is that the minute they stop HRT, their ability to make hormones will most likely revert back to its pre-HRT levels.**

Your body will only produce a certain amount of hormones, says Dr. Dorfman. When your body is functioning at an optimal level, you produce enough hormones to get adequate sleep, have a healthy sex drive, sweat a normal amount that doesn't require you to carry extra sets of clothing with you at all times, and not suddenly start sobbing when a toilet paper commercial hits you in the face.

HRT is used for a variety of reasons, from menopause, to transgender individuals who are transitioning, to medical conditions like hypogonadism in men.

"An individual's ability to make hormones after discontinuing HRT depends on the underlying reason for the therapy in the first place," explains Dr. Dorfman. Meaning when you stop HRT, your body then reverts back to its regularly scheduled programming. So, for instance, in menopausal women or men with actual low testosterone, their bodies have naturally decreased hormone production either due to aging or a medical impairment.

Discontinuing HRT will return those individuals to their pre-therapy low levels of hormones – it doesn't "kickstart" their systems to suddenly start producing its own hormones so they can eventually stop HRT and keep those higher levels of hormone production. It just means whatever your base level was before you started HRT, that's what you'll go back to when you stop.

As Dr. Dorfman notes, this is more common for someone who went on HRT for a hormone deficiency in the first place, because stopping HRT basically puts you back to square one – which in their case was not being able to properly produce enough of said hormone. It's not that HRT turned off the system per se, he notes, but that the system was already malfunctioning to begin with.

If you put a 70-year-old man with no testosterone production on HRT and then take him off it, the HRT is not going to magically reboot his system, as that system was already not producing testosterone. **HRT will supplement the lost hormone while he is using it, but it won't fix what was broken into working again.**

The Big Risk of Testosterone Replacement for Young Men

But, **if you put a 20-year-old man with healthy testosterone on HRT, there is a chance his system might not be able to naturally produce testosterone on its own if he supplements with hormones.**

But, **so many men are looking at testosterone as almost a form of performance enhancement and no one is explaining the risks to them.** And men aren't exactly known for talking about their health problems openly – or at all. There's an entire generation of men who have now grown up with telehealth like Hims for their more "embarrassing" health issues like hair loss and erectile dysfunction where they don't feel comfortable talking to someone face-to-face and they can just communicate from the anonymous safety of the screen.

Rebalance Does Something HRT Doesn't: Manage Cortisol

What's lost when people don't talk about these so-called taboo issues like menopause and low testosterone is people don't truly understand the risks of the treatments being prescribed to them, or that there are other options available.

Options like Rebalance, which can not only reduce symptoms associated with low hormones, but can also help support cortisol production. Because there's no such thing as HRT for cortisol, and one thing every person experiencing hormone imbalance has in common is skyrocketing cortisol.

When we studied menopausal women, one thing we noticed was that no matter when it happens, **menopause is extremely difficult, both physically and emotionally – a fact that is directly tied to your cortisol levels.**

For those dealing with medical menopause, the diseases they are facing not only place an extreme toll on their bodies, but on their emotional health. When you're facing a serious illness and navigating everything that comes with that – hospitals, insurance, understanding your illness and what it means for your future – that stress alone feels overwhelming. Throw early menopause into the mix and it's no wonder major depression can be a side effect for those experiencing menopause, especially if you have a history of depression in your past (Johns Hopkins Medicine, 2025).

For those women who go through natural menopause, it's by no means any less stressful. The perimenopausal and menopausal years are some of the most stressful times in a woman's life. She is usually at the apex of her career, with the most responsibility and stress she will have at her job. According to a recent British study, women over 50 are the fastest growing employment groups in the corporate world, with employment rates ranging from 55 percent to 67 percent across Europe, Australia, and the United States (O'Neill, Jones and Reid, 2023).

If she has children, she is navigating the complexities of raising children who are becoming exceedingly more anxious due to technology and social media. Her changing hormones and sexual desire may be causing issues with her partner that could be contributing to stress in her home life. And, if her parents are still alive, she is dealing with the realities of caretaking for them. It's no wonder that cortisol levels skyrocket – the same is happening for men, but the difference is they are not experiencing the rapid decrease in hormones that women are simultaneously going through at this age, so the symptoms don't feel as pronounced.

We have come a long way in how we talk about and treat menopause, but there is still so much more work to be done. Educating yourself about your hormones and your body is the first step to understanding how to treat your menopause symptoms. HRT, while safer and better understood, is still not a completely foolproof treatment option and should not be taken as the first line of defense against menopause symptoms.

Remember that cortisol also plays a role in menopause, alongside estrogen, progesterone, testosterone, and your thyroid. Managing your stress and getting better sleep through options like the Rebalance Hot Flash System, while also focusing on eating healthy, regular exercise with strength training to keep muscles strong, going to bed at the same time every night to get quality sleep, and alternative therapies like acupuncture can all have a helpful impact on your menopause symptoms.

Be Kind – Beating Yourself Up Won't Help

Most importantly, give yourself some grace during this time. Menopause is an extremely disorienting time – brain fog will have you misplacing your keys so often you might consider having them surgically attached to you. And your emotions are on a rollercoaster that will have you road raging in the Target parking lot one minute and crying because the barista spelled your name wrong on your coffee the next.

There is no logical response to this deluge of emotions because there is no reasoning with your body right now. As nice as it would be to have a magic pill that fixed all your problems, unfortunately that's not how whole system problems like menopause work. Be wary of anyone who promises to solve your symptoms with one pill or shot that works overnight. It took us over 40 years for our bodies to get to this point and it's going to take more than a day to fix it.

Patience isn't something that is in abundant supply right now, but try to muster some up as you navigate this exceedingly weird time – every day is going to feel like something new has changed with your body (Why do your ears itch all of a sudden? Is your skin supposed to be this dry? What's with the extreme lack of energy?), so the best way to get through it is to remember that you're not alone and you will eventually find the right treatment plan to get your symptoms under control.

Chapter 4

Stress, Anxiety & Clickbait: The Unholy Trinity Wrecking Your Hormones

Worrywart. Nervous Nellie. High-strung. Neurotic. Eldest daughter syndrome. The names may have changed over the years, but each of these somewhat derivative descriptors are ways that we've come to identify those who suffer with anxiety.

It's no wonder – pop culture has only just begun to treat mental health in a more representative way, creating rich and multi-faceted characters that those who are living with anxiety can identify with.

In the not-so-distant past, anxiety was often treated as a comic crutch. Think poor Cameron in *Ferris Bueller's Day Off* or the titular Bob in *What About Bob?* – the buzzkill that was always worrying about something going wrong and ruining everyone else's fun.

Except for a few outliers (*A Woman Under the Influence*; *Girl, Interrupted*; *The Virgin Suicides*; *Eternal Sunshine of the Spotless Mind*; *The Perks of Being a Wallflower*), it wasn't until the last decade that we've really seen a shift in how anxiety is represented on screen. No longer the comic relief or foil, anxiety is treated thoughtfully and with care, giving us well-rounded representations of what it's actually like to live with the different types and levels of anxiety.

From Jackson on *Sex Education*, a popular student and star athlete whose anxiety management fluctuates with his support system and medication protocol, to *Ted Lasso*'s titular football coach's debilitating panic attacks and subsequent working through his anxiety with the help of his therapist, we're in the golden age of mental health awareness and representation.

Not to mention the real-world representation of superstars like Simone Biles, Michael Phelps, Selena Gomez, Kristen Bell, and Demi Lovato speaking out about their own mental health struggles to let people know that it's ok to not be ok – which is crucial for allowing those who have anxiety feel seen. It also lets many people who don't realize they are suffering to identify that they might be one of the over 40 million adults in the United States that have an anxiety disorder (National Alliance on Mental Illness, 2025).

There has also been an uptick in services like BetterHelp and other online therapy models that make it easier for people to seek treatment as the mental health epidemic has grown and access to local mental health providers has become even more scarce.

The Difference Between Stress and Anxiety

To many, anxiety and stress may seem like one and the same. While both can cause you to feel unsettled and on edge, there are some subtle and not-so-subtle differences between the two.

Chronic stress is often associated with symptoms of fatigue or exhaustion, irritability, mood swings, changes in appetite, insomnia or sleep disturbances, chronic pain or headaches, digestive issues or stomach pain, and difficulty concentrating or memory issues.

Anxiety disorders, however, are often typified by symptoms of restlessness and nervousness, sweating or trembling, panic attacks, fear or dread, difficulty concentrating, aches and pains, intrusive thoughts or worries, avoidance of certain social situations or large crowds, a racing heart, and sleep problems, including problems falling asleep or staying asleep. See? – similar, but not the same.

But, perhaps **the easiest way to tell the difference between the two, according to Dr. Dorfman, is by identifying the underlying cause.**

"**The key differentiating factor is that stress is caused by an external factor,**" Dr. Dorfman explains. "Think back to your fight or flight response. Maybe you're walking down the street to take out the trash and suddenly there's a bear. The stress is caused by the appearance of that bear."

Rightfully so, I'd add. Dr. Dorfman notes that there can be other types of stress, like financial stress, relationship worries, work pressure – all typical external triggers that cause your cortisol to spike and your stress response to kick into gear.

Anxiety, on the other hand, has no distinct external trigger, says Dr. Dorfman. "There's no clear immediate danger to trigger that fight or flight response. If we use that bear analogy, with anxiety, you could just be lying in bed at night and are now worried that there might be a bear trying to get into your bedroom. It's a real trigger versus ruminating about something that might or could happen."

The same goes for non-bear related worries – **anxiety is worrying about what could go wrong in a situation when there are no indicators that anything is going to happen.** Maybe you had an argument with your spouse last week. Now you're up at three in the morning, panicked that they are going to ask for a divorce or that if they come home late they are cheating on you, or taking every sigh as an indication that your marriage is in crisis.

The same can be said for work – nothing sends an anxious person spiraling more than a less than stellar meeting with their manager. After that, every interaction, every message, every email, and every glance during a meeting is interpreted as the harbinger of doom for their career – the signal that they're about to get the dreaded, purposefully vague, "Hey, can I grab you for a quick chat?" message that every employee fears. The one that ends with their desk tchotchkes in a cardboard box and them morosely updating their resumes and switching their LinkedIn profile to #OpenToWork.

Anxiety, as you can imagine, is exhausting to both the brain and the body.

Why Stress Is Normal and Anxiety Is Not

While there's not always a fight or flight situation going on **with stress, there is a discernible trigger that you can point a finger at as to why you are feeling stressed out,** notes Dr. Dorfman. In other words, something caused you to feel that stress.

Anxiety, meanwhile, is worrying about something that may or may not happen. There isn't anything triggering you in the moment, but you are worried and fearful, nonetheless. People with anxiety tend to worry about the future or about situations that have happened in the past. They are worried about a recurrence of a past trigger or a fictional trigger that may not even exist in their life. It causes them enough anxiety that it interferes with their daily life – causing them to avoid certain situations, keeping them up at night, giving them panic attacks.

Another telltale difference between the two is that **anxiety doesn't affect everyone – while it is the most common mental health disorder, the underlying cause is still mostly undetermined** (American Psychiatric Association, 2025).

Researchers have narrowed the probable causes to a complex mix of genetics, chemical imbalances in your neurotransmitters and hormones, an unexplained increase in activity to the amygdala (the brain's processing center for emotions, including fear), traumatic events, and severe or long-lasting stress as all being possible contributors to the development of an anxiety disorder (Cleveland Clinic, 2025).

Stress, on the other hand, thanks to that Master Hormone cortisol, affects all of us, either in that immediate fight or flight trigger (the bear at the trash cans) or the more pervasive chronic stress (like the type one gets from not getting enough sleep and throwing their cortisol production out of whack night after night because they can't stop scrolling Instagram at two in the morning).

Dr. Dorfman also notes that, for the most part, **stress is a temporary response (excluding chronic stress,** which we'll dive into a bit later) which goes away after the threat or trigger has disappeared. **Anxiety is constant and more pervasive** – it's a condition that must be diagnosed by a medical professional who will then help to find the best way to manage your particular type of anxiety.

Stress – at least stress caused by an immediate trigger – says Dr. Dorfman is not a medical problem because it's a normal response to a situation. Your body is supposed to respond to a stressful situation with that release of cortisol (and, if the situation calls for it, adrenaline) – it's how your body protects itself. **It's when the stress doesn't go away and you are constantly stressed** – be it about work, relationships, money, family, or life in general – **that you enter that chronic stress state that becomes dangerous to your health and well-being.**

The Key to Understanding Stress, Chronic Stress, and Anxiety Is Whether Cortisol Returns to Baseline

To fully understand the differences between normal stress, chronic stress, and anxiety, you need to look at what's happening with your cortisol during each of these, explains Dr. Dorfman, specifically cortisol (of course) and adrenaline.

In a typical stressful situation, say, taking a test, your body will have a normal stress response, meaning that your cortisol will spike. After you finish that test, your cortisol will then return to its baseline and you will go back to feeling hunky dory about your day.

Now, say, during that test, a fire broke out in the classroom. Now, you've got adrenaline in the mix, releasing to put you in that fight or flight mode. Your heart rate is elevated, your body is on high alert because danger is imminent, and you are being told to run away from the smoking hot flames while the smoking hot firemen deal with it instead.

Because your cortisol spiked rapidly, as we discussed in Chapter 1 with our cortisol expert Alison Gracom, your body consolidated its functions to go into survival mode as it released that survival hormone of adrenaline to spur you into action and heighten your senses. Now you get to deal with that not-so-fun adrenaline crash – shakiness, exhaustion, feeling spent.

With anxiety, you know you have a test coming up, and in the weeks leading up to that test you become anxious about the outcome, worrying that you are going to fail. That worry snowballs and you start thinking about what that means for the future of your grades, your schooling, your potential career. You become so consumed with worry over this one test that you have trouble studying for it and might have trouble sleeping. You might do well because you're one of those lucky people who are just naturally good at taking tests, or you might bomb the test because you were so consumed with worry about it that you weren't able to focus on anything other than the consequences of what would happen if you failed.

As for where cortisol comes into the equation in all of this, scientists are still exploring the link between anxiety and the Master Hormone.

A recent study published in the journal *Biological Psychiatry: Global Open Science* sought to trace the role of cortisol in anxiety and major depression (Chan and Wu, 2024). Researchers analyzed blood samples of adults diagnosed with anxiety and/or depression taken between 6 a.m. and 11:45 a.m. to measure their morning plasma cortisol levels. **While researchers were unable to find any association between cortisol and major depression, they did find that elevated morning plasma cortisol primarily contributed to anxiety.** Basically, that if you have persistent, consistently high levels of cortisol in the morning, it could be a contributing factor to the development of anxiety.

More research is needed to understand if this development happens at a certain age – for example, are adolescents with chronically high cortisol levels more at risk to develop anxiety than adults or is it an equal opportunity causation? Scientists will also want to delve into how genetics, trauma, and the amygdala all play into the equation. Because not everyone with chronic stress develops anxiety, but it seems to appear that the majority of those with anxiety have chronic stress.

It's not surprising that researchers are becoming more interested in studying the effects of stress on our bodies – as a nation, we're becoming more stressed out by the day. And that's not hyperbole or commentary on the state of the economy or ruminations on how nasty the discourse has gotten on social media.

A 2023 Gallup poll found that Americans have been steadily reporting both sleeping less and stressing more since the early aughts (Fioroni and Foy, 2025). In 2003, 33 percent of Americans reported that they frequently experience stress in their daily life. In 2023 that number had skyrocketed to 49 percent. Conversely, in 2001, 54 percent of Americans said they got as much sleep as they needed. In 2023 that number dropped to 42 percent.

Sensing a pattern? This isn't your average trigger and response stress – this is chronic stress that is causing a disruption to our body's natural rhythms, interfering with our ability to sleep and reset ourselves for the day ahead. It creates a cycle that is unsustainable for our bodies, which in turn creates a type of modern dis-ease that we are unable to course correct from. And, at the root of all of this, is technology.

How Technology Robs the Anxious of Social Skills That Would Relieve Their Anxiety

For the anxious person, technology has been both a blessing and a curse. While it's opened the doors to provide them access to community and given them the resources to find tools to help cope with their anxiety, through therapeutic tools that can aid them with cognitive behavioral therapy (CBT) they may not otherwise have had access to, technology has also helped indulge some of their worst anxious habits.

Thanks to tech such as delivery apps and the advent of remote work and online communities, technology has allowed those with anxiety disorders to take their avoidance behaviors to the extreme, distancing themselves from social interactions.

What those without anxiety look to as convenience, like not having to talk to anyone on the phone when they want to order a pizza, someone with social anxiety is actually indulging in avoidance by relying on apps like GrubHub to completely bypass any sort of social interaction whatsoever, something many with this anxiety use to help them feel in control of their fears – a tactic that many psychiatrists don't recommend.

In fact, **exposure to their anxieties is usually a form of treatment that mental health professionals recommend to help decrease anxiety in the long term.** But, if someone is able to keep avoiding the situations that trigger their anxiety, they might never be able to break that loop. In contrast, they might actually deepen those anxieties – this a phenomenon that scientists call Pavlovian fear conditioning or avoidance conditioning, in this case meaning that **the more you avoid something to keep your anxiety under control, the worse your anxiety about that thing will get** (Beckers et al., 2023).

If you're anxious about the fact that you haven't been out on a date in a long time, so you avoid setting up a dating profile (or, you know, going out in the real world and meeting people), it becomes less and less likely that you will date. So you get more anxious about the fact that you aren't dating, but are paralyzed by inaction because you are so afraid of what will happen if you do, in fact, go out on a date. The cycle repeats and you are left fulfilling the thing you are most anxious about.

How Clickbait and Algorithms Ruin Your Life

But it's not just avoidance that technology has had an impact on. On the complete opposite end of the spectrum, **technology has allowed those with anxiety to see the absolute worst of the world** – whenever anything bad happens, a helpful little push notification pings its way onto their phone, alerting them to something bad, confirming their fears that there is danger in the world and they are justified in their anxiety. **And, the more they click into the stories and links of everything dangerous or scary, the more the algorithm serves them content that fits that narrative, reinforcing the anxieties.**

It's easy to believe your worst fears are all perfectly logical when the content being served to you just backs up that narrative. If you're scared of automobile crashes and you see a statistic that car collisions are on the rise, you'll click on that story to learn more. That will lead you into a piece that is crosslinked with more stories that back-up that statistic, which in turn might lead you to a Reddit community of people who have been in car crashes, who could then lead you down a rabbit hole of conspiracy theories about the automobile industry. Each new link leads you somewhere that only serves to reinforce or even amplify your anxiety.

To a degree, we have too much information and it's stressing us the eff out. Not just those with anxiety, but all of us. We'll talk more about the effects of push notifications in the next chapter, but having so much information at our fingertips, it can be argued, is not necessarily a great thing. Sure, we're more informed than our ancestors, but has that made us better people? What are the advantages of having all of this information?

The key questions here are what are we doing with the info we are obtaining and what is that information doing to our health?

Think about the news 50 years ago – there were four main TV news broadcasts to choose from in the 1970s. You could go to ABC, NBC, CBS, and (after the Watergate hearings) PBS to watch national news broadcasts each evening. Walter Cronkite was literally referred to as "the most trusted man in America" as he delivered the news each night from behind the desk at the *CBS Evening News*. There were very few "breaking" stories and those that were given that title truly earned it and the interruption into the TV programs they cut into to deliver the information.

Today, we not only have local and national news from the major broadcast channels, but we have multiple 24-hour news channels that deliver breathless "breaking" stories what feels like every minute, ratcheting up our blood pressure as they inform us of some new calamity, then devote multiple hours of programming to talking heads shouting at each other as they take opposing positions about said calamity and why the "other side" is wrong.

Watching these programs, no matter what your ideology or political leanings, feels as if they are engineered to ratchet up your blood pressure and get your stress levels through the roof in an effort to keep you from changing the channel until the next "breaking" story pops up and the cycle can repeat.

No wonder a 2023 Gallup poll showed only 32 percent of Americans have a great deal or fair amount of trust in the media's news reporting (Brenan, 2025).

We're suffering from information overload – there is too much coming at us from too many different sources, and it just keeps getting louder and more persistent. You can change the channel or turn the TV off, but your phone is going to keep pinging the information at you through news alerts and social media posts, making it inescapable.

It's no surprise so many of us are stuck in this chronic stress state.

The Differences Between Chronic Stress and Anxiety

The question then becomes, how do you know if it's chronic stress and how do you know if it's anxiety? The two can feel so similar, especially for someone experiencing it.

We've talked about the symptoms, and while they are technically different, there is some overlap. For someone who is dealing with anxiety, it can all feel perfectly logical to them and their actions easy to justify. The information you are receiving is skewing your view toward your anxiety and reaffirming your actions – not to mention the fact that everyone uses technology as a crutch these days to avoid uncomfortable situations.

According to Dr. Dorfman, when he's with a patient he suspects might be dealing with an anxiety disorder, one way he looks to see if it's chronic stress or if the patient should seek the assistance of a mental health professional for an anxiety diagnosis, is to look at what he calls the chronicity of the issue. In other words, **is it a chronic set of symptoms where they are experiencing the stress or anxiousness more days than they are not?**

"If you have difficulty controlling those fears, anxieties, or stress," he says. "If it's entering your life in ways that we wouldn't consider a societal norm, and it's impacting your work life, your social life, these are indicators of an anxiety disorder."

For instance, if your anxiety over cars means you won't drive, but where you live doesn't have any alternative transportation options and so now you are having trouble getting to work. That would be a situation where your anxiety has impacted your life in a negative way. **Dr. Dorfman also notes that if patients start reporting physical reactions to their anxieties – elevated heart rates, tunnel vision, breaking out in a sweat, feeling like they are going to pass out – those are all indicators that someone is unable to have a healthy stress response to a situation.**

When Stress Breaks Your Heart

Dr. Dorfman is particularly interested in the effects of anxiety on the heart because of a condition known as takotsubo cardiomyopathy (TCM), otherwise known as broken heart syndrome. This rare heart condition can be triggered by an intense emotional or physical stress and causes sudden chest pain and shortness of breath – it basically mimics a heart attack without actually being a heart attack. A part of your heart enlarges, but doesn't pump blood as well as the rest of the heart. Unlike a heart attack, there is no blockage in the coronary arteries.

With TCM, blood flow to part of the heart is blocked due to a temporary spasm or because the heart's smaller blood vessels don't get enough blood. Doctors still don't know exactly what causes TCM, but it's believed that an excess release of stress hormones, specifically adrenaline, could play a role.

Intense feelings of grief, fear, and sadness have been said to trigger TCM and having an anxiety disorder raises your risk for developing it (Oliveri et al., 2020). It's just one more example of how the more we feed our anxiety and chronic stress, the more we create a physiological response in our bodies.

We've come a long way in the last few decades of how we both talk about and represent mental health in the media and amongst our peers. It's no longer considered shameful to seek professional help to manage anxiety. But, chronic stress is often looked at as just another reality of the world we live in – an unavoidable part of existing in a fast-paced world. Some even wear it as a badge of honor, as if being perpetually stressed out and busy is a sign of achievement and success.

If you're not constantly hustling, how will you ever get ahead?

So we log more hours online, staring at screens to maximize our time, sacrificing our sleep – and, by default, our health – in the process. Our cortisol is constantly in a state of imbalance, which, eventually will cause us more health problems down the line if it continues to stay at those high levels.

There's a Path to Well-being

Anxiety and chronic stress don't have to be a foregone conclusion. Both can be managed with the right combination of treatment and habit changes. The most important thing for chronic stress is to regulate your sleep cycle and get yourself back to both the proper amount of sleep and going to bed at the right time to ensure that you aren't interfering with cortisol's natural highs in the morning and lows at night.

If you're glued to your device into the late hours of the evening, that's going to disrupt your sleep cycle and make it almost impossible to get that sleep you need, messing up your hormone production for the day ahead and setting you up for a high-stress day.

If you're spending hours of your free time staring at a screen, odds are good you're going to come across something that's going to stress you out (or, if you have anxiety, make you anxious) – so be more conscious with your screen time, or log off when you don't need to be online.

The more time you spend in the real world – especially doing things you enjoy with people you love – the better your mental health will be.

As we move into Part 2 of this book, you're going to learn more about the specific ways that technology has changed how you interact with the world and your fellow people.

While it may seem like we are more connected than ever, the reality is smartphones and other devices have actually created a communication rift that has led to loneliness, isolation, and a loss of intimacy between romantic partners.

As technology becomes more advanced, it's also becoming harder for us to resist its addictive pull – push notifications are just the tip of the iceberg. Your brain is slowly becoming hardwired to respond to the mere presence of a device, according to recent research.

The good news is there are ways to get your brain and your body back on track and learn how to coexist with your devices without letting them disrupt your sleep or your relationships.

Part 2
Technology: How Screens Are Frying Your Brain and Your Love Life

Chapter 5
Your Phone Is Smarter Than You Think— and It's Playing You

What's Worse Than a Phone Addict?

Paragliding, bouldering, downhill skiing – there is no shortage of extreme sports that can elevate your heart rate and give you a spike of adrenaline.

But, if you really want to test your ability to master situations that will try your patience, good nature, common sense, bravery, and problem-solving **there's one activity that is more challenging than any outdoor sport I've encountered: Going out with a phone-addicted friend who forget to charge their phone.**

Considering their device never seems to leave their sight and is so often in their hand it's basically another appendage, it can often boggle the mind how they manage to let it get to 0 percent when they use it to manage their whole life, but when it does happen, it suddenly becomes everyone's problem.

You know the type (or maybe you are the type) – everything is connected to their phone because they've so fully integrated technology into their lives it's as second nature to them as breathing. They don't carry a wallet because they have their ID and their cards saved in their digital wallet. They're constantly checking their front porch cameras whenever there's movement around their home.

Everything must be photographed or videoed and then shared on social media. They're texting multiple group chats even though they are supposed to be hanging out with you.

So, **when they run out of battery, suddenly you and your phone become their lifeline.** Can you check the time? Do you mind paying for this meal – they don't have any cards on them. What do you mean they can't go into this bar – clearly they're over 21 and why can't the bouncer just be cool about this?

They're really stressed about how their dog is doing and it's making them worried that they can't check their puppy cam, can you just try to be a bit more supportive right now in this trying time? What time is it again?

Will you take photos of the food and text it to them so they can post it on their Instagram? Oh, not that photo, that's a bad photo. Here, let them do it. That will have to do, but you really should get a portable ring light.

Can you text that group chat that you are both on and let them know about that thing you talked about a few nights ago? Why does your eye keep twitching like that? Can you call them a car? This night is kind of lame and they need to go post those pictures and check the group chat to see what everyone has been saying about that funny thing you texted for them.

It's exhausting being in the presence of someone who is constantly on their phone and it's even more trying to be in their presence when they don't have access to it.

When the Pocket-sized Phone Became the Pocket-sized Computer

Technology was supposed to make our lives easier, but instead, for many people it took over completely, making them dependent on pocket-sized computers they can neither live with, nor live without. It's a modern day catch-22.

Considering the multi-functional phone as we know it today really only became ubiquitous in the early 2010s – that is a phone with a built-in camera and wireless capabilities – it's astonishing to see how quickly it became such an integral part of our lives. While it's not technically impossible to exist without one of these devices, it does seem to make things extremely difficult in the modern world.

Take, for example, what happened in the restaurant industry after the COVID-19 pandemic was at its height. When restaurants re-opened, instead of going back to physical menus, many simply placed QR codes on their tables and asked patrons to scan them with their mobile device in order to view their options. It cut down on the staff having to wipe down each menu between service, and many guests found it convenient to be able to look at their phones if they wanted to order more mid-meal, rather than flag down a waiter. Except, of course, if you had made the conscious effort to not bring your phone with you to a social gathering, or had decided to be a person who owned a phone without wireless capabilities – it suddenly became an inconvenience to simply read a menu at a restaurant.

Many dining outlets liked the change so much that they continued the practice, even when strict COVID sanitizing protocols were lifted. If you don't have your phone or are still using a "dumb" phone, it becomes a production for the waitstaff to find you a physical menu, once considered the norm at any restaurant. Not to mention it encourages people to keep their phones out at the table, cutting down on in-person social interactions as we become distracted by what's on the screen in front of us. *"This conversation is really interesting; however I'm just going to quickly answer this text. And, oh wait, better check my emails really quick and make sure*

I didn't miss anything important. Oh, there's an Instagram message I need to just take a peek at while I have my phone in front of me."

Suddenly our IRL time becomes screen time and a quick catch-up with friends is just more of us looking at our phones while existing in the same space as our loved ones.

For a technology that feels like it's still in its relative infancy, smartphones have taken over our lives in a way unseen since the introduction of the automobile. And while it's easy to shake a fist at the clouds and blame society's ills on these tiny little gadgets, that would be disingenuous.

The Benefits Were Clear, the Dangers Were Not

Just as cortisol is not the bogeyman of the body, technology is not inherently evil and vilifying the device doesn't get to the root of the problem. Smartphones have made so many parts of our lives easier and, in some ways, opened up a window to the world that we can explore.

Unfortunately, we're too busy with our noses in our screens to do so. That's because technology has advanced at a rate that was far more advanced than humans evolve. Spoiler alert: We really haven't evolved that much, all things considered. It took six million years for humans to evolve from our ape-like ancestors, but the tiny smartphone evolved from the blocky brick portable telephone in a matter of decades.

No, the main issue with technology is that when developers created the smartphone, there were no discussions about how to responsibly use it before it was released to the general public. It's the same problem we saw a decade ago with social media and we're seeing now with AI programs where the technology is released and then everyone has to scramble to try and put the genie back in the bottle after the problems emerge.

With smartphones, we were simply handed a life-changing device and told "here is a computer that you can put in your pocket. The world is at your fingertips. Have fun!" Granted, **no one really understood or fully recognized the scope of the dangers of blue light, and social media had not become the all-consuming force it is today.**

Cyber-bullying existed in the bowels of AOL and MSN Messenger chat rooms, but we didn't spend nearly seven hours a day online (Kemp, 2025). It seems like an impossible number, but when you factor in time spent staring at our computer screen, tablet screen, and phone screen, those minutes start to add up.

Smartphones combined the addictiveness of the internet with the portability of a cellular telephone. What could possibly go wrong?

While digital addiction does not yet have its own designation in the DSM-5 (*The Diagnostic and Statistical Manual of Mental Disorders*), it is listed as a subcategory called out as an area of concern that needs more research before being considered a formal disorder by the American Psychiatric Association.

The World Health Organization, meanwhile, has identified technology addiction as a significant public health threat (World Health Organization, 2018). And, as recently as 2023, the US Surgeon General released an advisory that there is a growing body of evidence that social media is causing harm to young people's mental health (US Surgeon General, 2023)

All of which is to say, **evidence continues to mount that technology – especially excessive, unregulated use of technology, is harming our mental and physical health.** It's science confirming what many of us already suspected, but that we needed the clinical studies and data to prove.

Your Phone Is Smarter Than You Think—and It's Playing You

Smartphones Affect Our Bodies Like Nothing Else

The original purpose of the smartphone, however, was much more simplistic than the does-it-all device we rely on these days. Jo Lawson, a former Apple marketing exec, during the launch of the original iPhone and current CEO for Luum Precision Lash, was heavily involved in the marketing for the launch of the product. She notes that when Steve Jobs first envisioned the iPhone, it was meant to give you access to the internet, play your music, and be used as a phone.

"The App Store did not exist – I think Steve envisioned ways to use it beyond the internet in your pocket," Lawson says, "and I can't speak for him, but as someone who worked [at Apple], Steve was always about how does this make a customer's life better? It's a better way to use a phone, a better interface for the internet, better access to all your music, a better size. He was never about the hardware and always about what the hardware could do. He always said that content is king. Why these devices matter is because of what you can do with them. But, I think even he would be shocked to see the evolution [of the device]. I think he realized it would be a revolution, but not in the way that it has been revolutionary."

The phone itself, it seems, is not where the issue lies. It's everything that is now on it. Having a device that you can use to play your music, make phone calls, and browse the internet seems almost quaint by comparison. The advent of the App Store and allowing developers to create applications that we can add to our phone is where tech stopped being about convenience and started this path towards addiction.

Games, entertainment, social media, dating, shopping – if you can dream it, you can do it on your phone, for better or

for worse. That seven hours a day online number isn't looking so astronomical now, is it?

For some people, smartphones and tablets began to replace some of their traditional devices – a recent informal study of Gen Zs in the United States, Brazil, and France revealed that 50 percent use their smartphone to watch TV, 30 percent use their computer, 10 percent use their tablet, and only 10 percent use an actual television to watch their favorite shows (Broadpeak, 2024). In fact, compared to the rest of the population, Gen Z even owns fewer TVs than the rest of their generational cohort. According to recent data by the Consumer Technology Association, only 59 percent of Gen Z consumers personally own a television compared with 87 percent of total US adults (CTA, 2024).

While it's debatable whether staring at a phone screen for hours is better than staring at a TV screen for hours (I'm sure a spine expert may have some thoughts about which one is better for your neck and shoulder health, though), it goes to show that younger generations are relying on their phones as their primary device more than older generations. As the first truly online generation, it's no real surprise that they are more comfortable doing more online than their parents and grandparents before them – there was no adjustment period or switching from an "old-school" model to this new-school communication meets information meets entertainment hybrid.

But, at what cost to their mental, social, and physical well-being?

On its face, this progression from one type of tech to a newer type of tech seems like the natural progression of human ingenuity. As we become more advanced, so too will the tools we create to make our lives easier and more efficient. It's an inevitability of our species. And, just like with the Industrial Revolution and automobiles, as our species advances, the tools we create are going to have some unwanted side effects and health implications.

But, there's something different about technology, and, more specifically, mobile devices, that isn't shared by other advancements in our society. Barring perhaps (to a lesser degree) electricity, no other technological innovation has truly interfered with our bodies' own physiological rhythms in the same meaningful way as smartphones, tablets, and computers.

Take the blue light that emanates from all of the screens of those aforementioned devices. Artificial light is something that we haven't given much thought to because up until very recently it hasn't necessarily affected us in a meaningful way. But, up until the advent of the electric light, humans adhered mostly to the same schedule as that of the sun, following that natural diurnal rhythm. We may have extended it by a few hours with candlelight and fires, but for the most part, the majority of our day's activity was done during the sunlight hours, when our cortisol was at its peak, and we began to wind down as the sun set and our cortisol levels dipped, following that natural ebb and flow we discussed in Chapter 1.

Once electricity hit the scene, we were able to extend those waking hours for longer, yes, but many of us lacked reasons to stay up until the wee hours of the morning on a regular basis, past that 11 p.m. or midnight time when our cortisol levels were at their lowest.

Once the internet and portable computer technology became prevalent, suddenly we were easily connected to everyone. It might be 2 a.m. in New York, but it's 3 p.m. in Tokyo and someone else might be livestreaming or making content or posting. Might as well stay up and see what there is to see.

How Blue Light at Night Wrecks Your Sleep, Hormones, and the Next Day

Artificial light, also known as blue light, emanates from those screens as you stare at your phone or tablet and consume content.

While during the day, studies have shown that blue light can stimulate the parts of our brain that make us feel alert – clearly not an issue when you want to be awake – at night, this becomes problematic, especially before bedtime (Alkozei et al., 2016).

Daytime blue light exposure is actually helpful, improving your attention and performance. At night, it's not only disruptive, but actively harmful. Blue light affects your hormone productions, alertness, and sleep cycle. So that "harmless" scrolling through Instagram before bedtime or watching videos on your phone, or even reading a book on your Kindle app can all contribute to a physiological response in your body. **You're not winding down before bed, you're confusing your body's natural rhythms and creating a cycle that ultimately leads to low quality sleep, which, in turn, leads to higher cortisol and chronic stress.** Chronic stress, as we know from Chapter 1, can lead to a host of more serious health issues because of cortisol's role as the Master Hormone that helps regulate everything from our immune system to our brain health to our metabolism.

Blue light before bedtime, specifically the hour directly before that 11 p.m. cortisol drop-off, is the most dangerous. That's because that is when blue light interferes with your circadian rhythm. Specifically, it suppresses the release of melatonin, the hormone that makes us feel sleepy and increases cortisol (Lockley, Brainard and Czeisler, 2003).

Melatonin is produced specifically in response to darkness – when the brain senses it's dark out, it produces melatonin to encourage your body to start the process of winding down and preparing to sleep. But, **if you are looking at your phone and receiving blue light to your brain, you don't get that trigger because there is no sense that it is dark as far as your brain is concerned. This starts a cascading effect with your circadian rhythm that spills over to affect your cortisol production**, a process I outlined in

Chapter 2. All of this because you got stuck in a doomscroll on Instagram or couldn't stop arguing with a troll on Twitter or quit hitting the Next Episode button on the latest show you are binging.

As Lawson notes, studies on blue light's negative effects – or more specifically, blue light from devices, as the sun also generates blue light – was not something that was readily available during the creation process of the iPhone. So it's not as if the developers could have put in a safeguard to protect us from those melatonin-blocking wavelengths at launch.

It's kind of like seatbelts in the Model T – there were no studies about car collisions and keeping people safe from accidents with restraints because there had not yet been accidents to study and observe. Inventors like Steve Jobs and Henry Ford may have been visionaries, but they weren't psychics – the argument can be made that they had no true way to know what lay ahead as the inventions were merely tools and it is us as humans who make the decision on whether or not to use them responsibly.

"When engineers and designers and creative geniuses like Steve are inventing things, their integrity and their ideas are poured into the context of what they're making and other people spin off their ideas for good or bad," says Lawson. "It's like anything – you can use a knife to cut a steak or you can use a knife to stab someone. With blue light, there would be no history or data or way for us to guess that it would be something that would keep you up necessarily."

But, again, there were no guardrails put in place and the evolution of the technology moved so fast. Once developers realized they could create their own applications that could be integrated onto the phone, that's when things really started to get out of hand. It got to the point that the team at Apple saw the potential dangers and knew they needed to create an internal control to keep bad actors from using the device in a way that would create harm (oh, the irony). And so, the App Store was born.

"Within the first six months we were saying 'Ok, wow, we need to set up a kind of fence around being able to put something on the phone,'" says Lawson. "And the reason was that we were imagining some bad actors, and also we just wanted to control our brand. You're looking at it on an iPhone – do we want them doing whatever they're doing on an iPhone?"

With the App Store, Apple had to decide what the basic requirements were for each app to get approved to be in the store – what needed to be submitted in order to be approved, how long the approval process was, etc.

"We knew there were going to be third parties that were going to make [the phone] more valuable because of the work that they were doing. And we didn't ever want to do [that work], but we might want to include it, so what does that look like," says Lawson.

And developers and marketers were only too happy to provide all kinds of apps that in turn created all kinds of options and ways for us to engage with our devices, keeping us on them for longer and longer. There is no shortage of content to consume, and we are only too happy to continue with our pattern of conspicuous consumption.

A person could spend hours a day in a virtual world because the majority of these apps don't limit the time you spend on them. Why would they when most are run on ad spend and the more time you spend on them, the more ads you can be served?

Constant Push Notifications Put Cortisol in Overdrive

Blue light on its own would be damaging enough, and once we learned of its effects on our bodies' natural rhythms, there may have been a time where we would have found a way to limit our exposure, but once apps entered the picture and our phones became so much more than just a phone with songs and internet access, as was the original intention, there was no going backwards. Innovation only moves forward, after all.

But blue light isn't the only danger to our health. It, at least, has some positive effects.

The same can't be said for push notifications. Think about how often your phone buzzes, beeps, or dings at you. In the early days of smartphones, each of those vibrations or dings were tied to an alert that you most likely wanted to see – a text message from a friend, a phone call from a family member, an important email from your boss.

Now, practically every app on your phone is equipped with a push notification. Do you need to know that your favorite restaurant is running a takeout deal on dumplings? DoorDash seems to think so and is sending you a push notification to let you know.

Is it imperative that you are made aware that there's a new video from a retailer you followed once on Instagram to score a 20 percent off discount? Welp, it is now because you're getting a notification about it whether you like it or not.

And, like Pavlov's dog, each time our screen lights up or buzzes or chimes, we absentmindedly grab it to see if it's more clutter or something we actually want to give some of our precious attention to. Unfortunately, because everything and then some is on that tiny device, sometimes we end up staring at it for longer than the initial glance we intended.

Have you ever picked your phone up with one goal in mind, only to find yourself doing something completely different?

You might have meant to answer a quick text, but then a notification about a new direct message in your dating app caught your eye and the next thing you know it's an hour later, you've somehow wasted time scrolling through social media and added a bunch of new items to your online cart at your favorite shop, and now you're behind on a work project that was due 20 minutes ago.

Whoops.

Not only have you become distracted from the task at hand, **scientists say that just having the phone nearby while you are attempting to complete work makes it difficult to concentrate on what you are supposed to be doing, even if you aren't interacting with your device** (Stothart, Mitchum and Yehnert, 2015).

The mere presence of your phone is enough to take your focus off whatever you were working on and make your mind wander – even if you don't interact with your device. Is there any other invention in history that has that kind of power over us? To capture our attention just by being in our vicinity?

Notifications also trigger your brain's reward system, offering you a hit of dopamine from that sense of the unknown – you're not sure what that buzz or ding was for, but it might be something exciting or good so your brain has been conditioned to expect a reward and can't help but want to grab your phone to see what is on the screen (Betteridge et al., 2023). **This, in turn, leads to a constant state of stress** because you are perpetually on alert or feeling overstimulated by a phone that won't stop blowing up with dings and pings and vibrations, leading you to be overwhelmed by what turns out to be usually useless information from apps and advertisers (Yoon and Lee, 2015).

Reality Check, Please

Now, if you're someone who thinks that you don't spend too much time checking your phone and this doesn't apply to you, I've got some bad news: You do and it does.

While everyone is different, scientists estimate that the average person checks their phone 85 times a day, about once every

15 minutes or so (Andrews, Ellis, Shaw, and Piwek, 2015). Yes, that means you.

There's a reason Apple added the Focus and Do Not Disturb features to the iPhone to help people stay on task – we haven't been able to self-regulate and keep ourselves off these highly addictive devices on our own because we were never taught that there was a danger of addictive behavior in the first place. Or, that there was a way to use them responsibly. Instead, the technology was marketed as an "intuitive" user design. Intuitive to interact with, maybe, but not intuitive to disengage from and not have it disrupt your day-to-day.

Phone Addiction Is the Goal Because Your Attention Equals Profit

As these distractions pile up, so too does our stress and the possibility of sleep disorders. We already know just having it around you is enough to distract you, but even if you try to distance yourself from your phone, when it's your main form of communication, every buzz has you grabbing for it, just in case it's something important.

Studies have shown that there is a direct correlation between cell phone usage and push notifications – people will use their devices more and for longer the more push notifications that they get (Kim, Kim and Kang, 2016).

In some, this can turn into a full-blown smartphone addiction. For others, it just means you are exposed to information that you might not want to see.

We already live in a 24-hour news cycle. A lot of that information can be upsetting and divisive. While many of us choose not to keep news networks on our televisions all day long, our phones are sure to alert us whenever there is breaking news. And in this day and age, there is always some kind of breaking news – some fresh development somewhere in the world that someone out there thinks we need to be made aware of.

Just as the technology industry has evolved, so too has the media landscape had to evolve to keep pace. Algorithms and pageviews and metrics have all become the norm for news organizations, meaning in order for their stories to be seen and not get lost in the constant sea of information that you are bombarded with on a daily basis, everything from a headline to an intro needs to be written a certain way to appease both search engines and social media.

This leads to more frequent stories with more and more sensationalist headlines designed to get people to click on that outlet's version of the event. It's why when a major event happens, your news app suddenly seems to overload, blaring notification after notification of the same event, each with a more and more bombastic headline.

As you can imagine, this can cause a stress response and cortisol spike, particularly if the news is something troubling or personally triggering. A person can only be exposed to so much bad news before it impacts their mental health.

But, there's also a certain need to be informed and to have that information because it feels important and culturally relevant, especially when it is served directly to your device. You're not actively searching for it; however, it's been presented to you by a trustworthy source on a device you use to find information, so therefore it must be worth knowing. Not to mention, **as algorithms learn your patterns for clicking on certain types of stories, you will be served with the type of content you are most likely to click on.**

Cookies on a website sure sound warm and fuzzy, but as they gather data about you, they just continue to make it harder and harder to stay off your phone because all of your apps and websites just keep serving you content that it has learned through your history that you have an interest in.

It's a self-perpetuating cycle that builds upon itself, culminating with a population that is stressed out and so therefore unable to sleep, and unable to stay asleep and so therefore hindering natural hormone production and becoming more stressed out.

The implications of devices on our bodies are often spoken about as a personal responsibility – we're told that too much screen time can be dangerous for our health and that we need to curb it.

However, **when a device is strategically made more and more addictive through alerts and gamification, at a certain point, that line between what is possible for a person to physically be able to resist in a highly addictive product becomes extremely blurry.**

When developers keep making apps that are designed to keep you engaged for longer, creating a business model that lures advertisers in with the promise of engagement from customers, the stakes are high to keep people on their screens for as long as possible, continuously swiping and scrolling in the pursuit of more clicks and time spent online.

It's no secret that the more time we spend online, the worse it is for our health. But, we can't seem to disentangle ourselves from our devices, and that's not our fault – nor is it anything that is inherently wrong with the device itself. The problem is not that the technology exists. Again, the device is simply a tool that can be used as simply a combination phone and internet provider if that's how you choose to do so.

Where things get complicated is in the third-party apps and push notifications that are literally designed to grab your attention. It's the difference between passive and active engagement.

If you are actively using your phone, meaning you picked it up because you wanted to do something on it and you are engaging with it in the way you intended to do so, that behavior usually does not have an unintended effect on your cortisol. You grabbed your phone to do something you wanted to do and to look at something you wanted to see.

Of course, **with push notifications, there's always a chance you'll see something you didn't go looking for that could stress you out** – an upsetting news update, a text from your boss about an urgent deadline, an Instagram update from that one annoying person from high school that you still hate-follow who gets your blood boiling every time you see their name pop up on the screen. That's passive engagement, because now you're scrolling through their page getting more and more irritated by what you're seeing.

You picked up your phone to check the weather forecast, but somehow it's 45 minutes later and you're in a horrible mood looking at Becky from sophomore year's annoying over-the-top family photos in full cowboy cosplay in a pumpkin patch from three years ago. You don't know how you got here, you're angry at the time you've wasted, your blood pressure is raised, you're snapping at your partner, and you can't stop scrolling.

You would think that knowing what we know now, we'd approach technology with a more responsible attitude – studying its effects on our bodies before releasing something to the public with very little guidance or guardrails in place. After all, physiologically, we humans still are quite primitive from an evolutionary standpoint. We still follow the same cycles as our caveman ancestors no matter how many gizmos and gadgets we attach to ourselves in an effort to optimize our lives.

We need to eat, we need to exercise, we need to sleep, and we need to do that at a specific time to keep those systems performing at an optimal level or else cortisol rhythms will be disrupted and the whole cycle goes kaboom. But, our quest to innovate and our hubris lead us to believe we can create system-disrupting technology and release it into the world without protections and that people will just find their own ways to protect their mental and physical well-being.

AI Is the Latest Example of a Tech Revolution Without Safeguards

Look at AI as an example of the latest technology to be released from Silicon Valley without any protections for the unsuspecting public. You now have "art" being created by computers, writers being replaced with ChatGPT, deepfake videos and photos where people are having difficulty figuring out what is real and what is fake, and search engines integrating AI that is serving blatantly wrong information as the top return to a query.

When the creator of one of the most popular AI platforms is openly worried about the implications of artificial intelligence and the lack of regulation in the industry, clearly something is amiss (C-SPAN, 2023).

If this all sounds like a depressing dystopian novel for teens, that's understandable. Watching Silicon Valley race to create without considering the consequences has many people wondering what that means for the future. And what it means for the general public, while we wait for accountability from both the industry and the government, is that **the responsibility to monitor our tech consumption falls on us.** It's a minefield to navigate and requires constant vigilance, but **breaking the cycle of addiction to your device is truly a matter of the utmost importance for your health and wellness.**

While it's unrealistic to expect you to completely give up your device – and again, the device itself is not the issue – finding ways to monitor how long you spend a day on it, in which apps, for how many hours, and at what times, can be an enlightening way to see how your phone may be impacting your health.

Tips to Manage Your Phone Use

In order to best understand how to unplug, you first need to understand what it is you are doing with your phone. **The Screen Time function on your iPhone allows you to track the amount of time you spend each day on your phone, as well as where you are spending that time.** It also shows you what your most-used apps are, how many times you pick up your phone in a day, at what times you pick it up and how many push notifications you get each day and from where they are coming.

Take a minute to look at the Screen Time function if you haven't before and you might be surprised (or horrified) by what it reveals.

Go through a typical day for yourself and see exactly what that looks like for you, then jot it down using the following list so you can see what that looks like when written down on paper to truly understand the scope of both how much time you spend on your phone, where you spend that time, and when:

Screen Time Tracker data:

- Daily Total of Hours Spent on Your Phone:
- Time of First Pick-up of Phone:
- Last Pick-up of Phone:
- Most Visited App:
- Time Spent in App:
- Number of Push Notifications in a Day:
- App with Most Push Notifications:

- Hours of Sleep That Evening:
- Bedtime:
- Morning Wake-up Time:

Now, if you have kids, take a look at their phones and see what their screen time looks like.

The first step to get control of your phone use is to set your priorities.

To feel your best, the most important thing to safeguard is your sleep – as Gracom said in Chapter 2, by hook or crook, protect your sleep. The desire to have our phones near us at bedtime is a natural one. After all, not only do you have everything on there, it's your main mode of communication. But, knowing its addictive nature, that also means you are more likely to pick it up in that no-go time before bed and expose yourself to the melatonin-disrupting blue light and cortisol-spiking push notifications.

If you know you have no self-control with junk food, you don't stock your house with Doritos and Snickers. Likewise, **if you know that you have a habit of picking up your phone while you're in bed and scrolling into the wee hours, don't keep your phone on your nightstand or in easy reach. Make it hard to reach or inaccessible.** The easier it is to get to, the more likely you are to pick it up.

If you can't put your phone in another room, try keeping it somewhere in your bedroom that would require you to get up and out of bed in order to reach it. We tend to be lazy once we get comfortable, so the odds of you getting up to reach it at night once you've settled in go drastically down if your phone isn't right next to you.

To get started right when you wake up in the morning, no phone for the first 30 to 60 minutes. Instead, get going with 10 to 20 minutes of sunlight outdoors, drinking water, and moving your body.

Then **during the day, set blocks of time to focus on your work by putting your phone on "Do Not Disturb" and out of your sight.** Only allow notifications during blocks of time set aside for responding to them.

What are Smartphones Doing to Children?

Our next chapter is going to delve into how technology is affecting younger generations and their development – so much attention has been paid to the mental health portion of kids' interactions with technology, but have you stopped to think about the impact on their physiological development? I bet you have now.

Chapter 6
Why Kids Can't Sleep, Focus, or Play Anymore (Hint: It Glows)

Growing up in the age before cell phones was a unique experience – one Gen Alpha (born post-2010) and the generations that follow will never truly understand.

The freedom that most of us experienced during our childhoods is one that no longer exists in most parts of the world. Roaming the neighborhood after school with our friends, with no ties to our parents or home. Knowing that you could ride bikes or build forts or play kickball with the neighborhood kids until the streetlights came on (or mom or dad yelled from the front porch that it was time for dinner). Intricate games created from our imaginations and whatever was lying around. Despite having less to keep us occupied in the form of media, we found ourselves more creatively stimulated and more socially connected with our peers.

Gen X and older millennials might remember the phrase "It's 10 p.m. – do you know where your children are?" public service announcements that used to run on network TV late nights. It's hard to imagine the same type of commercial in the day of Find My iPhone and Air Tags allowing parents to track their child's every move, for better or worse.

While we might be able to argue that kids are safer and more monitored these days thanks to technology, they've also lost their ability to roam and feel a sense of unsupervised play, a crucial way that kids develop a curiosity about the world around them and develop social skills as well as increase their activity levels (ScienceDaily, 2007).

While it wasn't all idyllic, a childhood without the constant interference of technology had its benefits. **Children in pre-device years were better able to connect with their peers and were better at imaginative play** – they didn't experience boredom in the same way because they were better able to create their own intricate games when they ran out of structured activities. From building forts to creating imaginative worlds for their toys to devising intricate rules for nonsensical new sports, pre-device kids were extremely good at finding ways to entertain themselves because they had to be – there wasn't an endless supply of cartoons and iPad games to keep them occupied.

They also did not face the mental health challenges at the same astronomical rates that we are seeing today – a recent index created in partnership between the Harris Poll and the global impact non-profit behind *Sesame Street* found that **half of Americans described the average child as anxious** (Sesame Workshop, 2024). It's become an actual public health crisis and it's starting at younger and younger ages.

We Don't Know How Screens Affect Toddlers

Stressed out parents, unable to get their children to self-soothe, will hand over tablets or phones with games and shows for young children to watch at increasingly younger ages. No one has any idea what kind of impact giving children devices at such a young age will do to their developing brains and bodies.

But, when you are out to eat and your kid is screaming bloody murder at the top of their lungs and everyone is staring at you, the first thing on your mind is not, gee, I wonder if there is any physiological issue with little Jenny watching another episode of *Bluey* on her tablet. Frazzled parents just want some peace, everyone in the restaurant wants the tiny tyrant at the table in the corner to stop screaming so they can hear their dining companion talk, and the waiter would just appreciate it if the kid could just stop throwing fruit snacks at their head.

Besides, if everyone else is handing their phone over to their kids, it can't all be bad, right? Right?

The truth is, we have no real way yet of knowing what daily screen time for toddler ages will reveal because no generation has grown up with smartphones and content for children so readily available. Gen Z may have grown up in a digital world, but their exposure to devices at a consistent level truly began in their teen years.

Gen Alpha will be, for better or worse, the test generation where we begin to see how the constant exposure to devices has altered kids' development in mental, social, and physical milestones.

I'm not optimistic for what the science reveals based on what we are now beginning to see with Gen Z and their mental health.

This Is Your Child's Brain on Social Media

What we do know, based on what scientists learned from Gen Z and their interactions with social media, is that there's a direct connection between mental health and social media. This is a worrying fact when the Surgeon General's recent report on Social Media and Youth Mental Health reveals that 95 percent of kids aged 13 to 17 use social media and 40 percent of kids aged eight to 12 use some form of social media, despite most platforms having a minimum age of 13 to sign up (US Surgeon General, 2023).

Considering that brain development in kids aged 10 to 19 is at its most sensitive for determining self-worth, kids at this stage are extremely susceptible to comparison and peer pressure. Unable to recognize that what social media reveals is not necessarily the truth of someone's daily life, many kids experience depression and feelings of inadequacy because their life or image doesn't match what they see online.

Kids at this age are also reaching their peak in risk-taking behaviors, making the various challenges that pop up on TikTok all the more dangerous because it's children who are the ones that are most likely to attempt them. What seems like common sense to (most) adults – eating a liquid detergent pod is a quick ticket to the ER, climbing a stack of milk crates will likely result in broken bones, jumping out of a moving car to dance can lead to all kinds of injury or property damage – seems like nothing more than a fun way to be part of a cultural moment and get some likes and follows to impressionable teens. Many of these trends are appearance based and can lead to kids adopting eating and exercise habits that aren't healthy for their developing bodies.

Children Can't Tell Who Is Lying and What Is Dangerous on Social Media

With few legal limits around social media and kids and teens being the ones spending the majority of their time on those platforms, it's no wonder that we're seeing a crisis in mental health amongst young people. While social media can be helpful for adults to connect, network, and find community, kids and teens are still developing the parts of their brains that help them avoid the pull of peer pressure and allure of social validation through risky behaviors.

While we adults can (usually) recognize a filter and Photoshop on an image, teens may struggle to realize an image is heavily edited and wonder why they don't look like the photo they see represented in front of them. For as savvy as kids and teens are with technology, their brains are still developing and they don't yet fully grasp what is realistic and what is not. It's like the harmful diet culture of the 1990s and early aughts – when magazines would slim down popular celebrities on their covers until they were almost unrecognizable – but supercharged and with no guardrails in place.

There was a time in the 1990s when parents shifted from letting their children play unsupervised outside to a collective panic that kidnappers were hiding behind every parked car. Parents no longer wanted kids to be left to their own devices and kids were either expected to play outside with a parent present or indoors where they were "safe." Coincidentally, it was around this time that the personal computer became more common in American homes, and many kids got their first taste of the online world.

Adult Predators Target Children and Teens Online

Many parents may think that their children are safer online, protected from the evils of the outside world. While kids may be more insulated from physical harm (although, I'll argue later in this chapter that there's some debate to that point) when they are on devices, that doesn't mean they are necessarily safe. While a device may seem more inviting to parents because their child is physically present in front of them, and so, in theory, easily monitored, when kids are online, they are actually being exposed to more adult concepts than their parents might be aware.

Not only do kids lose out on many play-based social experiences that are crucial to their development in these pivotal years, but the odds of them coming across materials or concepts that are beyond their years means kids are growing up at an expedited rate.

Children can very easily find their way into adult spaces online, looking at adult content, or interacting with adults – oftentimes with their parents none the wiser about any of these scenarios. Besides being potentially dangerous to their mental health, these scenarios can force children to develop faster and introduce adult concepts at an earlier age that kids may be ready to handle.

You now have an entire generation (one could argue, two generations, as Gen Z was in their pubescent years when the iPhone was introduced) that were restricted in their real-life play but unsupervised in the virtual world. Is it any wonder a youth mental health crisis soon followed?

We were overprotective to the point of pushing kids away from the type of interactions they naturally needed to develop and instead shepherded them toward an online world that was full of a new kind of danger that none of us truly understood.

Kids Often Spend More Time Online Than Adults

You may be thinking, well, it's not like kids are spending the same amount of time online as adults, so the damage can't be that bad. After all, we have work counting toward our screen total and kids are at school, where oftentimes phones are prohibited during class.

As much as I wish that were true, unfortunately studies on device usage amongst children and teens has shown that kids are actually online as much or oftentimes more than their parents. **While we know that adults spend on average almost seven hours a day online, kids ages eight to 12 are spending on average four to six hours a day watching or using screens, while teenagers can spend up to nine hours a day on screens** (AACAP, 2024).

From interactive games like Roblox and Minecraft (two of the best-selling games of all time) to social media to streaming platforms like Twitch, kids and teens are constantly interacting online – with each other and their favorite influencers. **Oftentimes, parents may not know exactly what their kids are being exposed to – just because you might put restrictions on what your kid can access doesn't mean their friends' parents do, and they can see content that may be disturbing or age inappropriate.**

How Too Much Screen Time Harms Kids

Many a think piece has been written about youth device usage, social media, bullying, and mental health. It's important to draw attention to these issues as the effects will echo through young people's lives for decades to come, and we're still identifying the scope of just how damaging they will be as kids grow and develop into adults.

As technology evolves and kids adapt to the new online world, what will that mean for their mental health and overall development? **Some studies have shown that increased screen time leads to kids falling behind in key growth milestones like language, socialization, and emotional growth** (Muppalla et al. 2023). **This, in turn, can lead to a rise in health problems like obesity, sleep disorders, depression and anxiety.**

**Kids who spend too much time on their devices are unable to interpret the emotions of others, can't successfully socialize with their peers, are isolated, can become aggressive, and are more likely to have mental health disorders than those that have had limits set on their screen usage.

As those children become adults, those issues don't magically resolve and they suddenly become well-adjusted, emotionally regulated, socially adept, functioning members of society. If your emotional and psychological development is stunted at an early age, it creates a domino effect going forward as you mature into an adult who is unable to connect with others, gradually withdrawing from the real world and immersing yourself more and more into the online world.

These issues can't be taught away by a computer program or through a very special episode of *Sesame Street*. Elmo is good, but he's not that good.

Multitasking Shrinks Your Brain and Kills Motivation

We might believe that kids are ok to use their devices so much because of their high proficiency with technology and the relative ease in which a child can take to a device. After all, so many jobs in the modern workforce require adults to be skilled in any number of programs and devices that it stands to reason we would want our kids to understand and be adept at using those devices themselves.

A child who isn't intimidated by tech and able to seamlessly pick up and master new technology as it debuts is a child that will adapt to the changing world. Except, what's lost in that line of reasoning is studies have shown kids who spend too much time online do worse in school.

A Spanish research study found that kids who spent more time online had a direct correlation with lower reading proficiency and language skills (Peiró-Velert et al., 2014). They also had later bedtimes and a shorter duration of sleep, which we know can lead to a chronic stress stage and interfere with brain development at a key point in their lives.

This excessive media use meant a decline in academic achievement in testing scores, but the cause isn't necessarily just the use of screens – scientists think it can also be linked to children partaking in what they call media multitasking, that is, consuming multiple forms of media concurrently (Baumgartner et al., 2014).

If you've got the TV on while simultaneously texting someone on your phone or scrolling through Instagram or answering emails on your laptop, you're engaging in media multitasking.

Kids who regularly media multitask were found to have poor attention and executive skills – time management, organization, retaining information, self-monitoring, inhibition control, task monitoring, and, ironically, multitasking. These executive skills are all extremely important, not only in the working world but to be a healthy and well-adjusted adult.

Kids spend about 29 percent of their screen time media multitasking (Uncapher et al., 2017). As scientists begin to study its effects, they are discovering that it's creating a generation of young adults with poor memory, issues with impulse control, and even a physiological change in the structure of their brain. **Children with a high rate of media multitasking lose volume in their anterior cingulate cortex, the part of the brain that governs motivation, cognition, and action.**

Media multitasking can start as young as five years old, a fact that concerns scientists because of the amount of brain development that is happening during these critical stages. **Because children's and teen's brains are still developing, parents need to pay attention to not only how much screen time their children have, but how many screens they are consuming at once.**

Schools Battle Screens for Your Child's Attention

Schools have recognized that they are facing a unique issue with this tech-raised generation. Teachers, exhausted from having to constantly tell kids to stop watching TikToks or messaging their friends during class, have begun to crack down on phone use during school hours. It's a delicate balance, as parents – used to having 24-hour access to their children and worried about safety – insist on having their kids be reachable at all hours. But, **concerns about kids' mental health, plus new tech dangers with the explosion of AI, have forced administrators' hands and made phone bans more popular.**

But, **how do you monitor tech use in school when the children you are supposed to be teaching are more tech literate than the teachers, staff, and parents?**

While school-issued tablets and laptops are often used as learning aids in schools, many kids are savvy enough to have figured out how to bypass the school-installed filters and use the devices to access social media and games or hijack school messaging systems to send private messages and memes.

Schools might require kids to relinquish their cell phones during school hours, but that doesn't necessarily help cut down on screen time if kids are just finding ways to hack their school-issued devices to do the same things on their tablets and laptops that they would have done on their phones. And tech, as we've already explored in the previous chapter, evolves faster than humans are able to course correct and problem solve for the issues that it poses for our bodies and minds.

Just as schools were trying to figure out how to get a handle on device usage in the classroom, a more nefarious issue arose with AI-generated images. Reports of students using these programs to manipulate the likenesses of their peers into embarrassing or explicit situations began trickling in from schools across the country (Singer, 2024). This darker side of AI has obviously resulted in a new, more invasive form of bullying and assault. We are still in the nascent days of this disturbing trend, so we truly have no idea what the long-term ramifications will be; however, the immediate effects on teens' mental health and safety after being victims of AI-generated explicit images – especially teen girls – have left them feeling emotionally vulnerable and unsafe, both online and in real life.

Make Sleep the Top Priority

Setting limits to how much time kids can be on their phones and enforcing those limits while also fostering healthy habits together as a family can help course correct for when kids are not with their parents, giving them the tools they need to grow into healthy young adults that can self-regulate. Because, **even as we begin to scrutinize what screen time means for mental health, what's being left behind in the conversation is what devices are doing to kids' physical health – specifically, their impact on stress and sleep.**

Not only are kids and teens outpacing adults on device time, but to make matters worse (yes, worse than they already are), they also need more hours of sleep every night than we do – all that device time has to be coming from somewhere, and children tend to be scheduled even more than adults, between school, sports, homework, and activities.

The National Sleep Foundation guidelines state that **kids ages 3 to 5 years need between 10 to 13 hours of sleep every night, while kids 6 to 13 years old need from 9 to 11 hours of sleep a night and teens ages 14 to 17 need from 8 to 10 hours of sleep every night** (National Sleep Foundation, 2024). Yes, your teen constantly sleeping through their alarm is not unique to them – they really do need to sleep that much in order to feel refreshed in the morning and be alert for the day ahead.

We can't expect kids and teens to put in a full day of learning, plus develop emotionally, physically, socially, and mentally without the required rest the night before. And yet, we put a device in their hands, one that we ourselves can't regulate our own usage of, and expect kids to be responsible with their own time on it. The same kids that took a look at a dishwasher pod and thought, yeah, that seems like something I should eat on camera for internet clout.

Best Practices for Bedtime (for Your Children and You)

When looking for ways to cut down on screen time, putting a hard stop on devices after a certain time can be beneficial to everyone, not just to help limit daily hours online, but to protect your sleep and ensure that wind down is happening for you and your children as cortisol begins to drop in the evening hours.

Moderation and setting boundaries on screen time become particularly important for kids when it comes to setting rules around bedtime. Kids, after all, tend to have an earlier bedtime than adults, meaning that melatonin release needs to happen sooner for them.

Adults will want to cut out devices at least two hours before that cortisol drop at 11 p.m.; however, **with children often going to sleep as early as 8 p.m., that means screen time cut-off needs to happen earlier. In order to ensure the melatonin release is happening at bedtime, you can't have blue light interfering with that natural diurnal rhythm as darkness falls.**

While it's tempting to let kids watch videos on a tablet or play games or chat with friends on their phone while you unwind after a long day at work, **staring at a screen (and the blue light that emanates from it) right before bed will interfere with that** melatonin release and lead to shorter durations of sleep for kids who desperately need that rest for brain and body development.

And, if you think that cortisol ebb and flow is important for you, think about its impact on your child or teen. We know teenagers in particular are experiencing one of the most chaotic biological times in a person's life, when hormones are shifting at a rate that is only matched during menopause. **They need stability wherever it can be found, because internally, their bodies are going haywire.** Add to that a stress cycle completely out of rhythm due to late nights staring at a screen and you've got the same issues adults face, plus the added concerns of the cortisol imbalance potentially affecting the development rate of kids and teens.

We know how important sleep is to growing kids, and yet we give them often unlimited access to a device that has been proven to disrupt their sleep. Our own exhaustion and stress play a role, as fighting with our kids on how much and when they can use their devices is often more stress than we can take in our own days after battling disturbed sleep and daily stress – sometimes it's just easier to cave and enjoy the blissful silence that comes with a home that has children fully occupied by the screens in front of them.

After all, we reason with ourselves, they're socializing with their friends or watching something educational, so it can't be all that bad. We spent hours watching Saturday morning cartoons and playing video games and we turned out fine. Not to mention the fact that we are dealing with our own internal struggles with responsible device usage, after all, and it's a full-time job trying to get ourselves enough sleep to keep our cortisol regulated.

But, many of us didn't have childhoods dominated by screens in the same way – **if we're dealing with these types of serious** disruptions to our sleep now, the effects on children who are growing up with daily access to devices could make children more susceptible of maturing into adults that exist in that chronic stress state that Gracom warned about** in Chapter 1.

Granted, that type of diseased state that Gracom mentions would require extensive and prolonged exposure to screens that would have to be enough to completely throw our sleep cycle into a permanent dysregulation that would then put our cortisol so out of balance as to create those serious impacts to our other systems.

But, the fact remains that no one has a hard and fast number that they can point to and say, "If you start looking at screens at this age, for this amount of time a day, by this age you will have this impact on your health." We know that there is a possibility for it to happen; however, there are not enough studies or data to pinpoint a cut-off time or an age that is appropriate for kids to have access to screens, and an amount of screen time that is healthy for each age group.

Parents are left to make their best guess of what works for their kids with the little information that has been given, which is mainly, social media is hurting our kids mental health and too much screen time can be bad for kids' learning and developmental growth.

Until someone puts a clinically studied number on what "too much" really means, it's up to parents to decide what they think is appropriate based on their own daily usage of devices. And every parent has a different approach to what their child is allowed to do with devices. Does time spent on a school-commissioned tablet count toward that daily total? Does homework count? The answer is that no one has a true answer.

The best that anyone can do is what the American Academy of Pediatrics explains with its evidence-based approach when it says that it's less about the amount of screen time and more about the quality of the screen time, noting that parents shouldn't necessarily set a screen time limit for their children, but rather consider the types of interactions kids are having on devices (American Academy of Pediatrics, 2023). Their reasoning is that it's better to formulate household rules around communication, content, and co-viewing of what children are seeing online, rather than pay so much attention to the actual amount of time they are spending looking at screens.

I would argue that, knowing what we know about blue light interfering with melatonin production and cortisol spikes, parents should also be mindful of when kids are looking at screens. Attempt to keep devices out of your child's bedroom and have a cut-off period well before bedtime, so as not to interfere with their natural sleep cycle.

Moderation for the Win

It's almost a rite of passage for an older generation to bemoan the media habits of the generations that follow it. Rock 'n roll music was corrupting the youth of the 1950s and 1960s. Kids in the 1970s and 1980s watched too much television. The 1990s had parents in a panic about violent video games. The early aughts started the conversation around personal computer usage among kids and the dangers that could lurk online.

But, in screen time and devices, we've perhaps found a bogeyman worth being concerned about. Just as it is with adults, it's not that the technology itself is the issue, it's what kids are doing with it and how much time they are spending on it that is the real problem.

There's a long history of technology being used as a learning aid (shout out to the Speak & Spell, which taught many a 1980s child how to both spell and pronounce basic words) and that tradition continues today with many advanced games and devices aimed at teaching kids the fundamentals of education in a fun and interactive way. **Technology has been shown to have benefits for children** in a learning capacity, oftentimes aiding children who have a difficult time learning in some of the conventional methods (Haddock et al., 2022). And, when used in moderation, technology can facilitate peer communication, connection, and closeness.

The key word there is *moderation* – kids need limits on the amount of time spent using these devices and there has to be a balance between real-world interactions and time spent on YouTube, Discord, and TikTok. **Sharing memes and commenting on a livestream may be one way to connect with peers, but it can't be the only way that kids engage with each other and it can't take the place of in-person social interactions.**

Teens spend most of their online time watching videos – many of which are short and designed to quickly capture their attention before driving them to another video and then another. When the goal is to keep someone on a platform for as long as possible, it becomes difficult to enforce the idea of moderation.

Your Best Power Move: Set an Example

If you have ever tried to tell a child – be they a toddler, tween, or teenager – anything, you know that the one thing kids love more than anything else is being told not to do something.

In our heads, we imagine they see the very logical reasoning we are explaining to them, carefully consider it, understand it, digest it, and rationally decide that yes, that does make a lot of sense and they should stop doing the thing that we have calmly requested they cease doing.

The reality is the minute the word "no" leaves our lips, kids will do everything in their power to do the exact thing we just requested they don't do. Depending on the child, that could include screaming, crying, slamming doors, running away, hurtful language, glares, rude gestures, threats, pouting, sulking, sneaking around, and destruction of property – and that's just the toddlers.

It's quite literally part of their developmental process to push boundaries and challenge authority.

However, kids can't shoulder the full extent of the blame here. They are, after all, merely children. There's a certain layer of "do as I say, not as I do" happening when it comes to screen time. It's one thing to tell kids rules around device usage, but quite another if you don't stick to them yourself.

If you don't want screen time at the dinner table, but you start answering work emails or texts from your boss midway through Taco Tuesday, kids can't tell the difference between your work emergency and what is a crisis in their life.

While it might not have the same importance to you, to a teen, whatever fourth period dramatics went down between them and their friend group that day is the most important and devastating thing that will ever happen to them in the history of the world. There is no distinction for them and woe be the parent who tries to explain to their teen that their own problem was a "real" problem and their teen's drama isn't serious enough to warrant breaking the no phones at the dinner table rule.

Remember that when setting ground rules on devices, you might want to take a look at your own usage and see if there are ways to align your screen time with the rules you are setting for your child. If all they see is you with your nose in a screen, it can be difficult to preach moderation.

Considering we ourselves struggle with that same moderation, it can be an uphill battle trying to teach kids the same lesson. But consider maybe what moderation even looks like for you and your child. There are the necessary hours that you need to be in front of a screen (work for you, school for your child). But, when those obligations are finished, how much of your unwinding time needs to also be in front of a screen?

Your Children May Have to Ask AI How to Have Unstructured Play

Gen Alpha and the generations that follow are going to have technology and devices intertwined with their daily life. They learn on screens and are surrounded by tech in a way that the generations that preceded them could never have imagined. But that doesn't mean they are doomed to be antisocial, anxious, adults with short attention spans and high stress levels. In fact, some parents find that because their children are bombarded by technology from every direction, that they make a concerted effort to disconnect from devices and have meaningful time spent with the people they are closest with. Parents should foster that behavior in kids and teens, making sure to lead by example in the home with their own behavior with devices.

Finding opportunities to allow children the ability to have unstructured play, without a screen in the background, is not just good parenting, it's crucial to their development.

Kids need that type of free play that many of us grew up with in order to build creativity and problem solving skills that they will need in adulthood – skills they can't learn by watching a YouTube video or staring at a livestream of some Twitch gamer doing a streamathon of their favorite video game.

As much as we would like to believe that all those learning shows and math games are helping our kids to become baby geniuses, at the end of the day, we're relying on screens and raising a generation of iPad kids. What starts out as good intentions will lead to developmental issues down the road. As with everything else in life, the key is to strike a balance between helping kids navigate a world that is reliant on technology and the world of wonder, running around with our friends exploring until the streetlights came on that we grew up in.

Chapter 7

When 'Followers' Replaced Friends: Rebuilding Real Connection In Real Life

If there's one key thing that movies and TV shows of the 1980s, 1990s, and early aughts taught us, it's that all the best conversations between friends, family, or lovers happen over coffee. From *The Breakfast Club*, *Pulp Fiction*, and *When Harry Met Sally* to *Friends*, *Sex and the City*, and *Gilmore Girls*, some of the most beloved movies and shows of our formative years taught us that if you wanted to get philosophical, raw, emotional, or just rehash the wild times you'd had the night before, there was no better way to connect than with a cup of coffee and your closest friends.

From the eternal question of whether or not women and men could truly just be friends to the angst of being a misunderstood teenager stuck in detention, there was no problem too great that could not be solved by sitting together and hashing it out over a steaming cup of java. Enemies would become friends, friendships would deepen, and connections would be forged while sharing a mutual love of caffeinated beverages and whiling away an afternoon in a cozy coffee house as the world bustled by outside the windows.

What the Evolution of Starbucks Reveals About How Technology Wiped Out Our Real-life Gathering Spaces

Coffee shops in the 1990s and early 2000s played the role of gathering space for people to meet, hang out, and cultivate a community. Cozy chairs, inviting music, an almost living room – like aesthetic made people want to hang out and bring along their friends to connect over caffeine.

Nowhere was that more evident than with the early days of what started as a small, Seattle-based coffee shop called Starbucks.

When the brand first started in the United States, Americans didn't yet understand the concept of the coffee shop, notes Wendy Collie, the former senior vice president and general manager of US licensed stores, who joined Starbucks in 1990 under founder Howard Schultz, when Starbucks had a little over 100 stores in just four states. To Americans, used to diner sludge or their instant coffee in a can, the idea of 32 different varieties of whole bean coffee and a place to simply sit, drink that coffee, and hang out was as foreign a concept as whatever the heck a venti meant.

"The initial vision when I first started in 1990 had three things tied to it," says Collie. "Howard had gone to Italy and seen this sense of community surrounding espresso and felt like we were missing that in the States, along with good, quality coffee. But, more so it was really that he loved the fact that people stopped into their local place, got their espresso, saw their friends, saw their baristas, and then went to work. He felt like that was a huge gap in our society and he wanted to create that sense of belonging for people and part of their daily routine."

The second piece, Collie remarks, was providing good people with good jobs that actually paid good wages and provided benefits so that they could be a part of the fabric of the community.

That, in turn, led to the third piece, which Collie notes was the idea of creating an "environment where people had potential – where they could share in the success of the company."

All of this coincided with the rise of the so-called third place – a physical place between home and work where people could go and connect with their community. While in the past churches and community centers filled the role of the third place, in the 1990s, the coffee shop became the Gen X version of a third place – a modern, cool location where like-minded people could gather to exchange ideas, talk about music and politics and shared interests, to form new relationships and create community.

Starbucks, says Collie, tapped into that movement as it grew, creating spaces that customers were excited to linger in and that were hyper-local and targeted to the demographic. "People wanted more Starbucks and in 1995 we were only at 400 stores, but we had a vision of 2000 stores by the year 2000, which was a huge, lofty goal," she says. "Thinking about how to do that and create that third place became more of the impetus of how we designed the stores, how we hired people, how we trained people, how we made the coffee, how we were starting to engage with the communities. There was a lot of time and energy spent on getting to know people, getting to know their names, getting to know their drink, getting to know their dogs, getting to know their families.

"There was a tagline that we created somewhere in the late '90s that our mission was to uplift people's daily lives. So it became less coffee and it became more about the humans. And when we switched that conversation to uplifting people's daily lives, it switched the attitude in our store locations around how our baristas were interacting with our guests, because now they saw themselves as community members versus just baristas. That is how carefully evaluated the third place was in the early days. What kind of chairs? Where are the tables? Where do people want to sit? What are the sounds? What are they listening to? What are the mugs? How does it feel? How do people show up so that they are in a space of feeling uplifted. It was a very important part of strategy."

Soon, that commitment paid off to the peak Starbucks era in the early 2000s – the days of fireplaces, big squishy purple chairs, and an in-house music specialist cultivating mood music of the adult contemporary variety that customers could purchase as CDs that went on to sell millions and even win Grammys.

"We bought a music company out of San Francisco so we could produce our own music, because the music became so key to the experience in the store – on top of a barista knowing your name and your drink order," says Collie.

The company put so much emphasis on stores being a place for conversation and connection, that when the iconic Frappuccino debuted in 1995, Collie notes that while customers loved the drink, the baristas noticed an immediate problem in the stores. "Frappuccinos are not quiet. It was a real pain point for us because it created a different dynamic in the environment – you're constantly hearing the sound and it kind of stops people," she explains.

Rather than sacrifice the environment for the profit, the team created a shroud to place over top of the blenders and dampen the noise. "We had to put something over it so that it was quieter, because it was so loud, it was disrupting the ambiance, which disrupted the conversation."

If you walk into a Starbucks today, conversation is not something you hear much, if any of. Gone are the squishy chairs and the singer/songwriter music vibes. There are perhaps a handful of tables, maybe a somewhat soft chair here or there, depending on the location you are in. More likely than not, there isn't anyone inside the actual building and the majority of the customers are waiting in their cars in a drive-through line that snakes around the building. No one greets you by name as you walk through the door and your barista most likely does not have your order memorized and certainly knows nothing about your dog or your family.

The atmospheric shift, according to Collie, can be partly traced back to the advent of technology. Where once people waited in line for their drinks, chatting with those around them or the employees behind the counter, they gradually started to stare into their phones to answer emails and texts.

"When I first started, the lines would go out the door and around the corner by seven o'clock in the morning," says Collie. "And at that time, people were just waiting. What we found was, if someone was ringing at the register, but you're four people down the line, if we said, 'Hey, Justin, what do you want today?' They felt like service was really good. It was 'Oh, good – I know the line's long, but she sees me and she's going to get my drink started. I'll be out of here pretty quick.' Once technology kicked in, all of a sudden, you'd see they're texting, they're doing emails. And so what you saw was less dialog in the line. You saw less dialog with the register person. They'd get up and they'd just want to order because they're in the middle of something."

Collie notes that the decision to install free wireless internet at Starbucks locations created a change in the dynamic of the sitdown experience as well and was a decision the team initially wrestled with.

"Free wireless was a big deal in the late '90s, early 2000s," explains Collie, "so you had a lot of people taking a table and sitting there doing work for two or three hours. And there was a frustration that built for people who wanted to sit and have a conversation with their friend – there was no place to sit because everyone was at a table with single people with computers. That was a frustration point for customers, where they would see other customers hogging space on their technology and not leaving for a very long time."

Suddenly that comfy living room became less of a place to hang out with your friends and have deep and meaningful conversations and instead started to look like a type of remote office, where people were more concerned about finding an outlet to plug in their laptop than a cozy nook where they could post up and vibe with the music while they sipped their drinks and chatted about the meaning of life, the universe, and everything.

Looking into each other's faces while we forged connections was replaced by looking into screens as we connected to the World Wide Web. The microcosm of the coffee shop is indicative of a larger shift in our culture that has led to not only the loss of the third space, but a disconnection between people, even as we gather together.

Face-to-Face Interactions Make You Happy and Balance Your Cortisol – Until One of You Takes out Their Phone

It used to be that sharing a meal or a beverage with friends was the ultimate way to connect. But the next time you are in a bar, or a restaurant (or a coffee shop) look around at the groups that are gathered together. You'll notice many of those people that are gathered together are on their phone, not engaging directly with those around them. Oftentimes entire groups of people will all be staring at their screens simultaneously, the table quiet as they each perform a task, individual within the collective.

Technology, and phones in particular, have created a source of distraction so addictive that we can't pull ourselves away even when we are in the physical presence of those that are closest to us.

While smartphones can be an incredible tool to connect with those who we can't be with physically, sharing our thoughts or photos and videos of things we are seeing and experiencing, the use of them has become so prevalent in real-world situations that they've become a source of disconnection – it's hard to feel seen by someone when they aren't making eye contact with you or feel respected if they are too busy texting someone else.

In the information age, attention is truly our most precious currency and too many of us are not freely giving that attention to those that are most important in our lives.

If that all seems a bit sensationalized to you in the grand scheme of things – after all, does it really matter if you just check your phone while you and your friends are all out together? – then science has some bad news for you. **In-person, face-to-face social interactions are crucial for our well-being, particularly our happiness. Scientists have found there is a real mood-lifting effect present in face-to-face interactions that isn't found in digital interactions** (Monninger et al., 2023).

However, when, in the course of an in-person interaction, someone pulls out a phone and starts using it, studies have shown that both parties walk away feeling like the interaction was less enjoyable (Dwyer, Kushlev and Dunn, 2018). Participants report feeling distracted, less empathetic, and less friendly (Misra et al., 2014). The kicker is, **you don't even have to be looking at the phone – just having it out on the table or in your hand can make someone feel like the quality of the conversation is not as meaningful** (the whole distraction by presence effect again).

And happiness through those face-to-face social interactions helps directly affect our cortisol levels – studies have shown that social interactions help reduce stress-induced cortisol release (Ozbay et al., 2007). Social support also helps give people the coping skills they need to better handle stress as it manifests in their life, meaning **people who have a strong social** network are better able to manage and cope with stress as it occurs in their day, compared to those who feel isolated and without that support.

This technological disconnection is part of a larger, more systemic problem. We've become a culture of socially anxious, detached, extremely lonely people that feel unseen and misunderstood by our peers. We've lost the sense of community that binds us together and the skills necessary to build one by bestowing true, meaningful and positive connection that prioritizes the people we are physically with instead of the device in our hands.

When our attention is divided, it is impossible for us to create that type of deep understanding between people that allows them to feel truly seen and understood, making the interactions we do have superficial and lacking the depth needed to understand our closest friends, families, and acquaintances in ways that encourage them to be their truest selves with us.

It's gotten to the point that even when we are surrounded by people we feel alone.

In 2023 the Surgeon General declared a loneliness epidemic, with one in two American adults reporting that they experienced loneliness (Murthy, 2023). **People experiencing social isolation and loneliness are more at risk for health complications like cardiovascular disease, dementia, stroke, depression, and anxiety. It can also impact your physical health by making you less likely to eat healthy and exercise, as well as having an impact on your productivity, performance, and engagement at work or school.**

We're Still Recovering from the Effects of Social Distancing During the Pandemic

Of course, technology can't bear the full brunt of this social isolation. The COVID-19 pandemic fundamentally changed how we interacted (or, more accurately, didn't interact) with society. When the world locked down we retreated to the safety of our screens because it was literally not safe to be with those we loved. Zoom hangouts, Skype check-ins, HouseParties (remember that app?) – we tried more and more inventive ways to stay connected while being physically apart.

But, once the social distancing was over and the masks came off, it was like we had all forgotten the rules of gathering socially. Do we hug still? Are handshakes ok? How do you talk in a group if you can't just mute the conversation and turn off a screen to walk away when you don't want to engage anymore? It's as if all of our social batteries went from full power to perpetually half-drained, like the old batteries rolling around in the junk drawer that you're never quite sure are going to work in the remote but you feel like you have to jam in there and try.

But, when the world opened back up, one would think that the idea of looking at screens when we could instead look into the eyes of the friends we had been separated from would hold so much more appeal to us. **While many of us wanted to venture out into the world again, that time apart seemed to have taken what little social skills we still had and thrown them into a food processor.**

When most people think about having a conversation with someone, they think of sharing ideas or stories. **But a true conversation, one where both parties walk away feeling engaged, seen, and understood, is more than just connecting over shared experiences or ideas. It involves a mind shift that requires you to not** only be fully present in the moment and with the person you are speaking with, but to throw away the concept of efficiency and convenience and let the moment and discussion linger and meander.

Why an Efficiency Mindset Interferes with Our Friendships

Technology has trained us to subconsciously always be in search of convenience and efficiency. In theory, this is beneficial because it saves us time. When we save time on tasks we have to do, we are able to use that time to spend it on things we enjoy doing.

But that efficiency mindset is hard to break once you've become used to getting things done quickly and efficiently. Instead of truly listening to our conversation partner and letting them direct the flow of the topics and the talk, even if it means repeating a point for emphasis or a conversation that slowly meanders, we tend to cut quickly to the chase, or simply listen until we find an opportunity to volley back our own experiences or opinions, which can then make our partner feel unseen or unheard, compounding that isolation.

Can you truly be hearing what someone is saying if you are also thinking about how it relates to you or your life and how you can chime in?

Becoming conversationally illiterate isn't the only way that the efficiency mindset has created a social handicap for us.

Technology has opened the doors to so many different types of online communities that it has allowed us to curate our lives in ways that we can engage with the things that interest us and completely ignore those things that don't. **In the real world, we don't know how to disagree when confronted with people who don't share our worldviews or opinions and we don't actively seek out those with different life experiences to learn what we can** from them. It's alienated us in that we don't actively seek out new interactions or connections, making it difficult to expand or grow our communities.

What We Lose When Technology Replaces Real-life Encounters

That efficiency and convenience factor that technology adds to our lives means that we can also go about our day doing most everything we need online.

From shopping to banking to ordering food – even some doctor's appointments, everything we need can be done from a screen. **A person could go an entire day without ever speaking a single word aloud to another human being.** For a species that relies on social interaction for our mental and physical health and well-being, this isn't the flex that many think it is. Our brains have quite literally adapted to expect there to be others near us (Tomova, Tye and Saxe, 2019).

It used to be that every day required you to complete numerous tiny social interactions as you made your way throughout the world. From front desk receptionists, to chitchat with coworkers, to yes, a few pleasant words with your barista as you ordered your daily coffee, every day would bring small social exchanges with strangers.

Today, technology allows us to bypass those exchanges through online scheduling, work from home, and mobile ordering. While it's convenient, the argument can be made that it's not healthy and it adds to that loneliness epidemic as people move further away from human connection in their day-to-day lives.

What's even more concerning is that it's happening at every generational level as all ages become more accustomed to technology and adapt to its usage in their everyday life.

When many offices switched to a work from home or hybrid model after the pandemic, young people migrating into the workforce were given the freedom to no longer be subjected to long commutes and could live wherever made sense to them instead of where the jobs were, a definite quality of life improvement for many. However, they also lost out on a key social network that is foundational to many twenty-somethings. **Work friends, who typically can lead to larger networks in new areas and opportunities for socialization outside of the office through after-work drinks or meet-ups, are a core connection for young professionals just starting out in their careers.**

Without an office, these fresh hires also lose out on the opportunity to meet a potential mentor to help guide their careers forward and provide growth opportunities. Zoom, while being convenient, doesn't allow those young professionals the opportunity to observe higher-ups at work, watching their in-office dynamic and learning from those interactions. **Seeing someone conducting themselves in client meetings or feeling the excitement of finishing a project collaboratively helps new workers feel more connected and offers learning opportunities and professional camaraderie and the ability to potentially gain a mentor that they don't experience through a screen.**

Social media is awash with memes, earnest posts, and pleas from early twenty-somethings trying to find their tribe, and a recent survey reported that young adults are more likely than seniors to report feeling lonely – 79 percent of adults aged 18 to 24 versus 41 percent of seniors aged 66 and older (Buechler, n.d.).

Every age group is clearly struggling to make social connections, some are just better at coping than others.

We've become so comfortable being at home within our bubbles and not talking to anyone that the idea of exchanging pleasantries with someone on the phone while trying to order a pizza can create severe social anxiety.

Even something that should be a relatively safe social interaction, talking with your doctor about health concerns, has been co-opted by technology. Take, for example, the men's health company Hims, which has rocketed to success on the very simple concept that men do not like talking about "embarrassing" health concerns. Launched in 2017, the company quadrupled their patient consultations to two million by the middle of 2020.

Erectile dysfunction, hair loss, mental health – with a quick website evaluation and an online chat, men can order medication for issues they don't feel comfortable talking to their doctor about. Let that one sink in for a moment. We've gotten to a place where people don't want to talk to their doctors about completely normal health concerns and would rather go through a telemedicine company moonlighting as a slick men's lifestyle brand to be prescribed medication.

Putting aside the question of whether or not 20- and 30-year-olds even need to be prescribed erectile dysfunction medication – while there are certainly those young men who legitimately suffer from ED at a young age due to medication, stress, anxiety, obesity, recreational drugs, hormone imbalances, and poor sleep – a telemedicine survey that is reviewed and then approved by a remote doctor who never meets you in person doesn't get to the root of the issue causing the ED in the first place and instead offers a pharmaceutical solution based on a self-reported survey. **The fact that we have reached a place in our society where we don't even want to talk to doctors is indicative of a larger problem we as humans have with the simple act of social interactions.**

These little daily pleasantries we exchange with people around us may seem insignificant, but they are part of a larger piece of social connection that every person needs to build

community and ensure they don't feel lonely (Holt-Lunstad, 2017). The more social interactions you have with the people around you, the more likely you are to build community and to feel as if you are part of a community, which in turn helps you feel as if you are supported and seen.

Social Media Is No Substitute for Real-life Connection

Technology, and, more specifically, social media fools many people into thinking they are getting the necessary social connectivity they need throughout the day.

If you looked at your friend's Instagram feed and saw what they were up to for the day, that counts as catching up, right? Do you need to go out to lunch if you already know exactly how they spent their day? Apps like Facebook and Instagram fool us into thinking we have connected with our loved ones or fulfilled those daily social quotas because we are interacting with others.

But in-person connections are how we foster close friendships, especially when those friends are in the areas where we live. Social media is a helpful tool for keeping in touch with people we no longer are in close proximity to, or for finding groups of people with shared interests, but to truly connect on the deep, emotional level that humans need for our physical health, we need those in-person interactions. **Research has shown that while online connection is better than no socialization at all, people who have face-to-face interactions report a bigger positive mood boost than those who socialize via a computer screen** (Kroencke et al., 2023).

As we distance ourselves in person, it's leading to not only less physical time spent together, but a decrease in the physical size of our social network. Reports show that in 2003, the average amount of time that a person spent alone was 285 minutes a day or 142.5 hours a month (DiJulio et al., 2018). In 2020 that number increased to 333 minutes a day or 166.5 hours a month. Additionally, people reported that the number of close friendships they had also declined – in 1990, only 27 percent of people reported having three or fewer close friends, but that number has jumped to 49 percent as of 2021 (Cox, 2021).

One would think that as the world opened up to us via the internet, that it would allow our networks to grow, but we've only succeeded at shrinking our networks. **Sure, you have hundreds or thousands of "friends" online, but if you were to throw a party next week, how many people would show up?** If you needed help moving a couch, how many people could you call that would show up to help move it and share some pizza and beer with you afterwards to crack jokes about the experience and your bad knees?

Creating new networks is even harder in this digital age, as many people are discovering when they move to a new area. Relocating to a new city or town used to mean some disorientation as you found your footing and eventually found your people. But even with apps like Meetup, which offers hyper-focused groups that people can join online and meet at events in real life to find people with their shared interests – be it fantasy football, crafting, or board games – many people still struggle in new areas to make a new network of friends.

The allure of our couches and the familiarity of our screens coupled with this newfound social anxiety often outweighs the need for in-person communication. After all, if we're texting with someone, or swiping through dating apps, or hitting like on Instagram, it feels like we're interacting with someone despite them not being physically present. The problem with that, of course, is those interactions are generally quite superficial.

It's hard to muster up empathy when you are staring at a screen of text while *Love Island* blares in the background and your work computer and a half-written email to your boss sits on the couch next to you. **Can you truly be present in that moment and for that person if you are not physically with them?**

Think of any text conversation you've had with a friend that suddenly brought up something heavy – midway through did it turn into a phone call because the subject matter seemed too important to deal with over text? There are just some things that are too important for a medium that has cartoon emojis as a response option.

It doesn't help our cases that we use technology as a type of hybrid social crutch and lubricant all at the same time. Feeling uncomfortable at a party? Don't know anyone? Awkward lull in the conversation? Pull out your phone and start texting someone you know or scrolling through your emails and no one will bat an eye. It gives you something to do so you don't feel alone but you don't have to stand against the wall grasping your cup and feeling lame.

The irony of that situation is that you are quite literally surrounded by people that you could approach and enter into an actual conversation with instead of retreating to the comfort and isolation of your screen, but there is a risk with talking to a real, live person that doesn't exist online. We can control what happens and where we go and who we engage with online. If you don't like the reaction to your post, you simply go elsewhere.

In the real world, you have to deal with the awkwardness of small talk and views you might not share and misunderstandings. But there are also potential new friendships and love of the same obscure British sitcoms from the 1980s and deep dislike of artificial grape flavor.

In the same vein, our phones also serve as a type of social lubricant when we are trying to connect with someone over a topic but can wind up derailing the connection.

How many times have you referenced something and pulled out your phone to use as a visual aid? Or queried a fact and then whipped out your phone to Google it and prove your point? Knowing what we know about how the mere presence of the phone can serve as both a distraction and make the conversation feel less empathetic and participants less connected, is it really worth it to prove a point?

Does anyone really care that much if the *Muppets Take Manhattan* came out in 1984 or 1985? Or if the correct turn of phrase is champing at the bit or chomping at the bit? Do you care enough to devalue the connection with the person in front of you in order to prove a point? We've become so accustomed to having the world at our fingertips that we've taken for granted what's right in front of our faces and it's actively doing harm to our well-being.

Simple Steps to Reclaim Your Real-life Social Skills and Community

In an age where people take to apps like Reddit with impassioned pleas of feeling alone and looking for friends to just grab a drink or watch a movie with, where the crucial third place has disappeared and community involvement is at an all-time low, **how are we supposed to get back to the social interactions we so desperately need as a species?**

The easiest answer is to put down the phones and to leave our homes. Engagement in our communities – through volunteering, through neighborhood activities, through activism, through recreation – is only possible if we actually step away

from the screens and make a concentrated effort to engage fully with people in real life.

That means keeping your phone out of your hand and out of sight when you are with people because of its ability to distract and take away the value of an interaction with its mere presence.

But creating community, both strengthening the existing social network that you have and building a new or bigger one, means dedicating time, energy, and – most importantly – focus on creating those bonds. It's one thing to want deep, emotional connections but that requires putting in the work to do so.

Instead of trauma-dumping on poor Elmo's Twitter feed with our existential dread and loneliness, we need to go out into the world and talk to a real, live human (Fish, 2024).

Start small if the thought feels overwhelming – instead of a mobile order for your coffee, give yourself an extra 10 minutes in the morning and go inside a Starbucks, stand in an actual line, order from behind a register, and engage in small talk. Don't pull your phone out as you wait in line, but stand and observe what's going on around you. Continue that pattern for the rest of the day.

Open yourself up to interactions that could not normally happen if you had headphones on and your face in your phone. Will they all be pleasant? Absolutely not. But life seldom is. You may, however, stumble across something or someone you might not have noticed if you had been staring at a screen instead.

By making an effort to engage with people around you, there's a possibility of making a connection. There is, of course, an ample opportunity for rejection; however, there's a 100 percent chance of rejection and loneliness if you don't attempt to broaden your social network. **Walk around your neighborhood, greet your neighbors, find community centers, learn ways to get involved, frequent your local restaurants and chat with the people there.** If you're new to the neighborhood, use that as a conversation starter and ask for advice on places to go – if there's one thing people love, it's giving opinions.

As for the conversations themselves, be an engaged participant that makes someone feel listened to. It pains me that in the twenty-first century we've reached a point where people don't understand the art of conversation, but there's more to talking to someone than simply nodding along, looking interested, and waiting until it's your turn to talk.

To get the most out of a conversation, you need to be a good conversation partner. That means being an active listener who gives both verbal and physical cues that they are engaged in the story being told by their conversation partner – nods, facial expressions, direct eye contact, encouraging affirmations.

It's also a good habit to get out of the efficiency mindset when in a conversation with someone. Does someone repeat a point or a feeling in their story? Do you circle back to something that was already covered once before? **It's ok if the conversation meanders instead of going straight to the point – sometimes we need to sort out how we feel about something or repeat a particularly emotional point to help us feel seen or understood.** It's not a race to get to the end of the story. Building on that by asking follow-up questions if someone is talking about something that you can see is important to them.

People generally feel bad about talking about themselves for too long or too much, especially with someone they've just met. **Asking follow-up questions gives them the permission to speak more about a topic that excites them or a story that is dear to them because you've specifically asked for more details and shown that you are interested.**

And, remember that a conversation is not a performance or a job interview. You're not trying to wow them with how impressive you or your life is. You aren't showcasing a picture perfect existence for anonymous likes and follows. **There is no need to try and outdo someone or "top" their story with your own tales of woe or achievement.** In our attempts to try and build a connection, sometimes we shift attention back to ourselves instead of simply listening and letting the person in front of us feel seen and heard.

These lessons become extremely valuable for our well-being and in helping us to effectively manage stress (and, by default, keep those cortisol levels in balance), but also play a role in our intimate relationships. If you think technology upended your social network and how you interact with friends, it's just the tip of the iceberg when we look at its impact on your intimate relationships.

Chapter 8

Dating Apps Are Designed to Keep You Swiping (Not Satisfied)

Dearly beloved, we are gathered here today to mourn the passing of the meet cute. The plot set-up of numerous rom-com movies (and basis of most of Meg Ryan's career), the meet cute created so many of our favorite fictional couples in a whirl of happenstance, kismet, banter, and precision timing. From Kate Hudson's Andie and Matthew McConaughey's Benjamin in *How to Lose a Guy in 10 Days* to Richard Gere's Edward and Julie Roberts's Vivian in *Pretty Woman*, the meet cute leaves behind a who's who of iconic couples in film.

Unfortunately, the domination of online dating in the real world meant the slow demise of the meet cute, as the concept of randomly meeting and then dating a complete stranger is so foreign of a concept to most young, modern audiences that the meet cute was seen as unrealistic, contrived, and trite. Flowers (red roses only, naturally) can be sent in care of Anne Hathaway, Reese Witherspoon, Sandra Bullock, and Jennifer Lopez.

Ok, that might be a bit dramatic – Hollywood has a longstanding love affair with the meet cute as a plot device for romantic comedies and as long as somebody keeps rebooting franchises and remaking classics to capitalize on nostalgia, the meet cute will always have a place in cinema.

But, more and more of the audience now exists in a world where dating, especially the start of a new relationship, is initiated online – making the idea of casually bumping into someone at the grocery store while you absentmindedly reach for the same gallon of oat milk – or your dogs tangling you up in their leashes – or making a bet that you can do everything women do wrong in a relationship to make a man dump you, while he simultaneously makes a bet that he can make you fall in love with him over the same 10-day period – less and less likely for young daters (alright, maybe not so much that last one).

The Real Goal of a Dating App Is to Keep You Addicted to the App and Single

When dating apps first arrived on the scene back in the early aughts, they seemed like a revolution in dating. **Unlike online dating websites,** which had a (somewhat unfounded) reputation for being a last resort option for desperate people who were unable to meet potential partners in the real world, **dating apps made online dating seem normal and cool.**

I actually met my wife on a dating website back in 2000 when there was still a stigma attached to online dating. Despite the fact that our first date lasted 14 hours and I found my soulmate through eHarmony, it was considered uncool in those days, so I would spend hours making up wild and romantic stories of how we met so that when people asked, we would have something to say that wasn't online dating because I knew the kind of looks we would get despite how natural and solid our connection was. The stories got more and more outlandish and we would laugh at every silly meet cute I devised.

Today, that shame doesn't exist, mostly because **apps are the primary way that many single people date. They're efficient and gamify the dating experience to allow singles to feel as if they are achieving a goal when they log on.** You could see hundreds of matches and get all the chit chat out of the way before wasting your time on a date in real life. Filters let you weed out people who didn't share your values or were outside your age range or location, so you could focus in on potential partners who fit your criteria. **Dating began to feel like a game, with a swiping action that created quick dopamine hits whenever you got a new match. Our brains like looking at pictures of attractive people and they really like it when those attractive people also find us attractive** (Klucharev et al., 2009).

In theory, apps made dating so much more efficient and targeted – instead of getting dressed up and going out in hopes that you might meet someone who you hit it off with, you could go online and swipe through potential matches that you found attractive and whose profiles explicitly stated their hobbies, interests, background, and if they shared the same relationship goals as you.

Whether you were in search of a long-term partner or here for a good time but not a long time, dating apps created a sense of control and offered you choices that you may not have found while sitting in a bar on yet another Friday night wondering if it was too late to join a nunnery or monastery. Scrolling through profiles from the comfort of your couch as you flirt with potential matches and set up dates, it seemed as if the world was your dating oyster.

However, gradually, as time went on, we discovered that for many of us, there was no pearl to be found diving through the apps. While some downloaded the app and eventually found their person via a Tinder swipe or Bumble match, countless others have become disenchanted with the coldness of the apps and the endless swiping.

And, like many other facets of technology, **science has found the darker side of dating online with the addictive quality that has been engineered into the very DNA of these apps.** There's an unpredictability to dating apps that promotes the reward centers of our brains – you might not have the apps open, but users are still looking at your profile. So, when you come back from a hiatus of looking at Tinder or Hinge or Bumble or Grindr, you may find you have more matches or likes than when you last looked, despite you not being active on the apps.

You don't know what you may find when you open the app, and that type of unpredictable reward (McClure, Berns and Read Montague, 2003) provides a greater surge of activity in the reward centers of the brain than rewards that we know are coming – basically **your brain is more stimulated by the chance that something good might happen rather than knowing you are going to receive a positive outcome from working hard to receive the reward** (O'Doherty, 2004). It makes dating apps extremely addictive (and the entire idea of "a dating app that's made to be deleted" completely farcical) because you can't help but go back into the app for more potential gratification.

Who knows if there might be a highly attractive person at the next swipe, or if you might have a potential new match from a hottie in your inbox the next time you log on? Your curiosity gets the better of you and keeps you coming back for more.

When you are out in the real world, looking around a room shows you exactly what the options are for the evening – you're not going to go to 15 different bars in one night and talk to 50 different people in an attempt to find the best match for you. That's exhausting just to think about, let alone attempt. **Online dating has turned the act of finding a partner into a numbers game where everyone thinks their perfect match could be just one more swipe away.**

Of course, if you're not finding the love of your life on the apps, this can also lead to an increase in cortisol spikes from thinking that maybe the issue is you when the reality is that it's how the apps themselves are designed. Your brain doesn't know the complex algorithms are made to keep you swiping – you just know you've gone on yet another lackluster date and your inbox is full of potential situationships instead of the true soul connection you've been searching for. It's bound to stress out even the most emotionally well-adjusted and rational dater.

Besides the obvious problems with endless swiping, **the human brain is ill equipped to deal with an abundance of choice.** If you've ever walked down the cereal aisle at a grocery store and been so overwhelmed by all the colorful boxes that you freeze and panic grab a box of Cheerios, you understand that sentiment. **Attempting to date via apps can lead to a case of choice overload that leaves you feeling stranded** in the cereal aisle, awash in choices and unable to make an actual decision. **Studies have found that when confronted with less options, people tend to be more satisfied with their choice – too many choices can lead to decision paralysis.** In the case of dating apps, that has led to what we now know as ghosting (Iyengar and Lepper, 2000).

Online Dating Anonymity Allows Confidence-crushing Behaviors Like Ghosting

The phenomenon of ghosting – connecting with someone on an app, maybe even going on a date or two, and then cutting off all communication with absolutely no warning or explanation – has become an all too common occurrence in the dating world to the point that it's become an expectation. An inevitable, albeit unfortunate, toll that one must be willing to pay as the price for the convenience of dating via app.

A 2018 study revealed that one-fourth of respondents had been ghosted by someone, while one-fifth had they themselves ghosted someone else (Freedman et al., 2018). Because the apps provide a sense of anonymity – we are not linked to those we match with through our social circles – the real-world consequences of dating and ditching aren't ones that we need to concern ourselves with because the likelihood of us ever crossing paths with the ghostee are few and far between.

But, as anyone who has ever been on the receiving end of someone they were starting to develop feelings for (or just an inkling of a flirtation with) pulling a disappearing act, there are some very real psychological and emotional ramifications of being ghosted. As the phenomenon has become a certifiable trend in dating, **psychologists note that those who have been ghosted report feelings of confusion, rejection, and lower self-esteem** (Navarro et al., 2020).

Ghosting can also lead to long-term effects of cynicism and mistrust toward future partners that spill into future relationships, causing people to anticipate a potential partner is too good to be true or going to go full Casper and ghost them at a moment's notice, creating a cycle of low self-worth and self-sabotage.

It's hard to trust someone on the other end of a screen after you keep having people unmatch from your dating apps with no warning or explanation after what you may have thought was a good date. It causes you to question not only your judgment, but yourself and your potential as a partner.

The Habits You Develop in Online Dating Do Not Lead to Relationship Success

Even without emotionally cruel behaviors like ghosting or breadcrumbing (leading someone on with flirtatious, but non-committal messages when you have no intention of actually dating them), **online dating can be an extremely stressful and emotionally fraught environment that does not lend itself well to true intimacy.**

Dating apps may have expanded the dating pool and made it feel as though there are more opportunities to connect, but **the reality is there is less depth in those connections and people are not as satisfied with the connections they make** – mentally, emotionally, and intimately (Hobbs, Owen and Gerber, 2016).

When the dating experience has been both abridged and gamified, distilling your core into a photo to be judged and swiped on, people begin to focus on finding the perfect photo and an attention-grabbing bio that will get them a match.

Intimacy in a relationship is about feeling close to someone and connected to them – physically, emotionally, intellectually, and spiritually. **It's impossible to find that type of true intimacy in dating when an interface has been designed to be photo-driven** in an attempt to make it as easy to view and potentially match with as many new people as possible without having to scroll through big, chunky blocks of texts that tell you lots about them.

The founders of these apps might claim they designed them to take the stress out of dating, but what it really feels like is as if someone took that horrible Hot or Not website from the early aughts, made it location-based, and added a messaging feature. While there are people who have been able to find true intimacy and their person, it sometimes feels like it was in spite of, not because of, the design of these apps.

If you talk to anyone who is single and on a dating app, odds are they have a mostly negative view about them – that they are a necessary evil that are worthwhile for hook-ups,

but not very useful for anything real. Because once those butterfly feelings of infatuation with a new romance disappear, if you don't have intimacy, you're going to start getting turned off by the quirks you once found charming very quickly. A strong, healthy relationship is built on true intimacy – not a mutual agreement that the other is hot.

Not to mention the fact that the more time we spend looking for love in the digital world, the less time we devote to face-to-face connection in the real world (Nie and Erbring, 2002). We know social media – despite expanding our network – actually makes us lonelier, but dating apps create a false sense of intimacy. How can we be lonely when we have so many people interested in us? But because **online dating is replacing dating in the real world, rather than supplementing it, we spend less time focusing on pursuing real-world connections.**

Singles are disillusioned with dating apps – you hear the refrain of "I'm getting off the apps" from your single friends on a near daily occurrence – but **when faced with the reality of dating offline, the social anxiety of meeting someone who hasn't been pre-vetted or filtered out by algorithms often proves too overwhelming, sending them right back online.**

We're addicted to the comfort of apps, which tricks us into thinking the sting of rejection isn't so bad when it's not face-to-face. What no one tells you is that the bad parts of dating aren't the only thing that get dulled in the digital world – you also lose out on the highs that come from starting a relationship in the real world because you are not only constantly chasing that reward sensation of new matches, but also you aren't creating the types of deep connections that come with real-world intimacy.

Why You Need to Stay in Touch with Real-life Friends (Literally)

Many singles, after yet another Tinder date gone wrong, joke about giving up on modern dating entirely and just staying single. While there's certainly nothing wrong with that – and, in fact, many people have found fulfilling lives without a partner – **it's important to ensure you have a robust social network you can rely on to fulfill both your intimacy and physical touch needs.**

No, not like that – according to Gracom, recent studies have revealed what many of us probably already subconsciously suspected after spending time with our friends and loved ones when we are feeling stressed or anxious. "One of the things that helps balance cortisol is oxytocin – the Huggy Hormone," says endocrinology expert Alison Gracom, PA-C. **Physical touch helps release oxytocin, which not only makes you feel all warm and fuzzy inside, but has also been shown in numerous studies to impact your cortisol levels as well.**

Researchers in a 2021 German study discovered that participants who were exposed to a social stressor and who then received a 20-second hug from a research assistant experienced a statistically significant reduction in cortisol secretion compared to the control group (Dreisoerner et al., 2021). In other words, **when exposed to a stressful situation or stimuli, the act of physical touch can actually reduce our cortisol levels.** Researchers measured cortisol via saliva, and were able to track cortisol recovery back to baseline at a faster rate than those in the control group.

Now, a few things to note here – this particular study also had a group that self-soothed, giving themselves a hug. That group tracked the fastest recovery back to baseline. The theory some psychologists have is that because the German study used hugs administered by strangers, people might not have been as comforted by the physical touch as they would have been by a loved one or romantic partner.

A previous study in 2017 found that self-stroking (easy, tiger – that means placing your hand over your heart or stomach with gentle pressure in a gesture of self-soothing or giving yourself a hug) was not as successful at stress reduction or satisfying as being touched by a romantic partner (Triscoli et al., 2017).

Think of a time when you were upset or stressed – if you were in a relationship at the time, your most natural instinct was to reach for your partner's comforting embrace. A hug, a clasped hand or quick reassuring squeeze, a soothing back rub could all work wonders to not necessarily heal your pain or erase your stress, but to alleviate the severity of what you were feeling and make everything feel more manageable in that moment.

Affectionate touch from a partner can help to alleviate feelings of loneliness, anxiety, and depression, lowering our heart rates and cortisol levels as it simultaneously releases oxytocin – everything from foot massages to back rubs to hugs to simply holding hands can create this effect and strengthen intimacy between partners (Schneider et al., 2023).

This doesn't mean the touch is necessarily a prelude to a sexual encounter, but rather a way to strengthen the bond between couples while giving comfort and providing physiological relief to the stress of our modern day (Ditzen et al., 2007).

When couples aren't physically bonding, they are not only creating a rift in their relationship, but they are unintentionally missing out on the stress-relieving benefits that their mere physical presence can have for their partner. Jojo and I call each other our charging station – no matter how stressed or sad we feel, the second that we have physical contact (be it holding hands, leaning on each other, or even just our feet touching in bed), we both feel an instant calming and peaceful effect. A bad day can be erased by an embrace when we are reconnected.

While there are positive benefits to self-touch when we're feeling stressed or overwhelmed, for those who are single and fed up with the app-based dating world, finding ways to ensure you are getting that necessary oxytocin release (and the subsequent cortisol drop that follows) are imperative to your overall mental, emotional, and physical health.

However, you don't want to be that person that starts randomly hugging someone in the produce aisle at the grocery store because you're not getting the physical touch human beings as a species need. It's not just weird – you're probably going to end up on the news or possibly with a not-so-friendly visit from the authorities.

That drive to connect with others, and, specifically for physical touch, means that those who are not in relationships need to be diligent about both cultivating new connections and bolstering existing ones. Technology is not helpful in that respect – a 2019 study found that when people are even just holding a smartphone, they are less likely to smile at others (Kushlev et al., 2019) It's kind of hard to make friends and look open to conversations when you don't look very friendly.

COVID Social Distancing Made Us Afraid of Hugs and We're Still Recovering

It doesn't help that it's gotten harder and more fraught to even have casual physical contact these days. Just as the pandemic impacted our working relationships and friendships, so too did lockdowns and social distancing impact how we approach and greet others.

Where once we may have shook hands or even hugged strangers or casual acquaintances as a form of greeting without any thought to it, those simple actions carried very real consequences in the days when no one was quite sure exactly how COVID-19 was spread. It was drilled into our heads to stay away from each other and to not touch anyone for the safety of ourselves and the greater good.

Even after the worst of the pandemic passed, the new, unspoken rules of good social decorum state that you don't initiate touch with someone if you don't know their level of comfort with physical touch.

While the worst of COVID-19 may be over, we still have people who are immunocompromised, people dealing with long COVID, and people experiencing PTSD from what we collectively went through as a population during 2020 that haven't been able to put the habits of lockdown behind them.

Maybe that's why products like weighted blankets, cuddle pillows, or adult swaddlers suddenly surged in popularity – we craved the comfort of physical touch that we were unable to access during that very scary time. Those popular products simulated the sensation of being hugged or cuddled for those that were unable to be with a loved one who could offer that type of physical comfort.

Many of us took those casual handshakes and shoulder touches and back pats and friendly hugs for granted, however, and now that they are no longer the norm, we're seeing what happens when people stop being polite and start getting real – sorry, had to do it, the mood was too heavy.

Real World shout-outs aside, **there is promising new research that demonstrates that the type of touch and the relationship of the person touching you is less important than previously thought.**

In a large-scale 2024 study that explored the impact of touch on the stress levels of newborns, children, and adults, **researchers discovered that – as far as adults go – the person touching you, how long they touch you, and the type of touch doesn't actually** make a difference in terms of significance on the impact of your mental and emotional health (Packheiser et al., 2024).

A quick hug from a close friend had the same impact as a long-lasting massage from a research assistant. Granted, you're not usually in a situation where you are getting consensual massages from strangers while waiting in line for your coffee – if you are, are you sure you're at a coffee shop? – but **the study reveals that those congenial back pats and those "sorry, I'm a hugger!" greetings from new acquaintances have a more beneficial impact on us than we may have previously given them credit for.**

Meaning that as they disappear from our daily lives, the impact on people who do not have romantic partners at home or who are not dating regularly could be more serious for loneliness, depression, anxiety, and stress than we previously realized.

Again, that doesn't mean we get to completely ignore others' boundaries in the quest for more balanced cortisol and better mental health; however, **those who are single – especially if they are pausing their dating attempts – should be aware of their daily touch interactions and strive to find opportunities for intimacy with friends, family, and loved ones on a regular basis.** And, if a handshake or a friendly hug is offered (and you're comfortable accepting it), that casual moment of touch could have more benefit for your mental well-being and cortisol levels than you realized.

Couples Can Read Their Phones Together and Still Flourish with This One Weird Trick

Single people aren't the only ones who can fall victim to this loss of intimacy in a digital dating age. Established couples of all tenures, be they married for decades or dating for months, can also find themselves experiencing less intimacy in their relationships due to technology.

For some couples, especially working couples with kids, the mental exhaustion of just getting through a day can leave them completely drained of what little social battery they had.

Whether they go to an office or stare at a Zoom screen all day, interacting with co-workers, dealing with parental duties, making sure the kids are entertained (while, hopefully, trying to keep them off screens – hint, hint), all can mean that when it's just the two of them at the end of the day, the idea of sitting down and having a deep, meaningful conversation to build intimacy is enough to send them running to the comforting glow of their screens, sitting on opposite ends of the couch as they swipe, tap, and scroll in blissful silence.

Modern love is sending your partner a funny meme on Instagram, while you veg out in your designated comfortable spot of choice, with a TV show playing in the background that you're both only half watching, asking how each other's day was, then retiring to bed to continue scrolling on your phones until one of you passes out and asks the other to turn out the light. Not exactly the stuff of the classic rom-coms we grew up with.

No wonder the erotic fantasy romance (and the sub-genre lovingly referred to as "fairy smut" by its die-hard fans) novels are one of the fastest growing categories of fiction right now – women of all ages are escaping into the sweeping epics with their intense leading men and headstrong heroines with their "soul bonds" and intense intimate connections to fulfill the intimacy that's missing in their real lives, oftentimes due to a combination of our busy lives and our addiction to technology.

Think of how irritated you get when you're out with friends and they are distracted from your conversation by their phone.

Now, **think about what it does to your blood pressure when you're trying to have a conversation about literally**

anything – from taking out the trash to a topic that interests you – **and your partner is only half-listening because they are on their phone.** It definitely doesn't do great things for your intimacy or your relationship as a whole. **In fact, there's even a (extremely unwieldy and awkward) word for it: Phubbing, a portmanteau of "phone" and "snubbing."** Yeah, it's not great, but then again, neither is the act of phubbing.

A 2021 study found that **phubbing (yup, still awkward) had a direct correlation to relationship satisfaction,** with those couples where one partner used a phone in the presence of the other reporting feelings of exclusion, less perceived partner responsiveness, and less intimacy for an overall more negative relationship satisfaction (Beukeboom and Pollmann, 2021).

Interestingly enough, the study found that the issue itself was not conflict over phone usage or jealousy, but rather one partner feeling excluded and removed from the other partner's life.

Researchers found that when the phone-using partner (the phubber) involved and informed their spouse (the phubbee) about what it was they were doing on their device, those feelings of exclusion and lack of intimacy decreased and there was a noticeable improvement in relationship satisfaction.

So, **it is possible to use your phone while in the presence of your partner, but the key differential is that you need to include them in your scrolling** – talk about the article you are reading or the meme that is making you giggle or the news story that is making your face scrunch up in that weird (but adorable) way. Instead of sending it to them without commentary and continuing your endless solitary scrolling, tell your partner what you are looking at and have a discussion with them about it in the moment.

Even better, do so while cuddled up on the couch while engaging in some form of intimate touch – a caress, a hand hold, taking turns with foot or back massages. Connecting both physically and verbally is a guaranteed way to help reduce stress while also boosting intimacy, rather than siloing ourselves off to unwind with time spent completely apart.

Studies on phubbing have also revealed that the quality of conversation was impacted, with phone users being viewed as less polite and attentive, as well as the quality of the conversation between a phubber and a phubbee as one of lower quality than when a phone was not present (Vanden Abeele, Antheunis and Schouten, 2016).

It's hard for someone not to associate their partner's attention to a screen as a way of ostracizing them, seeking the attention of others, or finding them not being "worthy" of their partner's attention. This can not only hurt the relationship, but lead to issues with self-worth and self-esteem. While the phubber may just be obliviously reading a news story or answering an email from their boss, their partner could be spiraling out with feelings of inadequacy as a spouse, thinking they are no longer attractive or interesting to their partner.

Phubbing also leads to less responsiveness, something every relationship needs to build and foster deeper intimacy.

If you tell your partner that you are having a tough time at work or are feeling overwhelmed with the kids' activity schedule or that menopause is giving you hot flashes that make you feel like an alien from a lava planet has possessed your body, your hope is that your partner will respond with full eye contact, empathy, and a supportive conversation that will make you feel understood, validated, and cared for.

What you really don't want to get is a non-committal "uh-huh" as they shovel cereal into their mouth, never taking their eyes off their tablet as they scroll and tap occasionally on the screen. The lava planet alien possessing your body just might erupt and start shooting heat beams out of your eyes in fury at the lack of any emotional response or support.

In order to truly have the intimacy our relationships need and to increase relationship satisfaction, we need to prioritize taking the time out of our busy days to connect with our partners, both verbally and physically, on an intimate level that helps us continue to learn and grow with each other.

Now, to be fair, the idea of sitting down with your partner for a full-fledged conversation after you just spent the entire day talking to co-workers or teachers – or arguing/pleading with your children to do something or not do something (that they then most likely proceeded to not do or do) – might sound absolutely exhausting.

You might prefer the idea of just sitting alone, untouched and completely non-verbal for some very precious me time instead. I don't want to discount the importance of carving out some quiet time for you to recharge your own mental, social, and emotional batteries.

But, that should not be at the expense of your relationship.

There has to be a balance in which you are able to prioritize both and not sacrifice one for the other or half-heartedly do both – staring at a screen silently while you are in each other's presence does not count as "quality" time together. Couples are starting to realize that without deepening their intimacy and focusing on emotional, physical, intellectual, and spiritual connections together, their dissatisfaction with their relationship will only grow.

While, ideally, we would spend our downtime off of all of our screens and fully engaged with those we are with, those types of behavior changes can be too much for many people to tackle all at once.

The overall goal is to work your way up with small changes in your patterns that can help boost intimacy between partners and strengthen your overall communication for a healthier relationship as a whole.

Considering that the national divorce rate sits at 42 percent (National Center for Health Statistics, n.d.), and many of the remaining intact couples report low levels of satisfaction on one or both partners' behalf, finding any ways to ensure that you can build intimacy, and, subsequently, relationship satisfaction, will only benefit both partners in the long run (Bühler, Krauss and Orth, 2021).

But, **when 70 percent of couples report that they feel that cell phones interfere with their relationship, it's a pretty solid indicator that screen time is detrimental to the intimacy** we are trying to build in order to be more satisfied with those partnerships (Sbarra, Briskin and Slatcher, 2019).

Coupled with the increase in cortisol that the presence of screens can activate, it adds up to partners who are disconnected and stressed – not a great start for keeping the spark in a relationship alive. So, if you must incorporate screens, make sure you are actively engaging with each other – be it playing a video game together, talking about what it is you are looking at on your phone, physically touching each other while watching a movie, or taking breaks during your screen time to check in with each other and have conversations about what you are viewing or a topic that interests you.

Without intimacy, relationships will not grow and evolve positively.

Scientists have been trying to discover for decades what the secret sauce is for success in a marriage – they have no empirical evidence to say what will make one couple last over another. There are too many factors to consider when a relationship starts that impact a marriage.

However, **I truly believe that intimacy is a key indicator of not only how strong a relationship is, but also how emotionally and physically healthy both partners are and how satisfied they will be in a relationship.**

Communication is one of the biggest stressors between partners and technology has not done us any favors in that department. As couples grow together and their relationships evolve – maybe children, job changes, location, financial struggles, health problems, aging – the more they are able to communicate with each other and face challenges together as a united front, the stronger their foundation will be to get through both good times and bad.

Attraction and common interests only go so far for so long – growing together means fostering deep intimacy at every level, emotionally, physically, intellectually, and spiritually. That requires putting in work, even when you are exhausted and feel stressed and overwhelmed. Because the irony there is that **taking the time to connect with your partner, especially if you have been building that foundation of intimacy, will actually help alleviate those feelings of stress and anxiety.**

**You might think that sitting down with your phone and quietly scrolling Instagram or texting your friends is the best way to unwind, but the not-so-funny joke is that particular pastime – especially if you're engaging in it at night, alone, while in the presence of your partner – is elevating your cortisol in the long run by winding you up before bedtime, suppressing your melatonin release, and interfering with your sleep cycle, with an added bonus of making your partner feel like you are ostracizing them or that they have low self-worth. So much for a relaxing evening routine.

Dating Apps Are Designed to Keep You Swiping (Not Satisfied)

Real-life Dating Is Coming Back Because It Works

As for those singles still figuring out how to date in an app-based world increasingly set up to keep them single, it might be time to make good on your threats to get off the apps in your quest to find love.

The makers of these apps, despite their claims of trying to help people take the stress out of dating, are, at the end of the day, running a business. They don't stay in business and make money if you find your true love and delete their app forever.

That might not be how they started, but it's what they've evolved into, and while the people on the app may (for the most part) be genuine in their quest for real connection and intimacy, the platforms have created a mindset that addicts our brains in a way that we can't control.

So, proceed with caution and be sure to be looking for opportunities to date in the real world – as more people become disillusioned with apps, we're beginning to see a return of dating in the real world. **Singles mixers, speed dating, meet-ups, activity groups with shared hobbies, and plain-old going out with friends with an openness to meeting new people is making a return among people of all ages.** And, along with it are success stories of people finding connections with real intimacy, mostly because they started through more than just looking at a photo and pithy bio.

Above All, Get Connected in Real Life and Stay in Touch

If you've decided to take a break from dating for a bit, or just want to focus on living your best possible life and not be constantly in search of someone to complete it, remember the importance that your social networks have and prioritize cultivating and caring for those connections with friends, family, and loved ones.

Don't forget to emphasize physical touch and make a point to both self-soothe and find moments to initiate and receive that cortisol-regulating physical touch on a regular basis. Just please, don't go hugging strangers in the grocery store, for everyone's sake. And, if we could all agree to never mention the word "phubbing" again, I think that would be for the best.

Dating Apps Are Designed to Keep You Swiping (Not Satisfied)

Part 3
The Reset: Less Doomscrolling, More Doing

Chapter 9
Suck It (Literally): How Our Lozenges Help You Un-frazzle

If someone handed you a brightly colored gummy, its crystalline sugar sparkling like diamonds in the sunshine and its happy neon hue inviting you to take a bite, you'd rightfully think you were eating candy.

If that person told you that the delicious, sugary treat you had just eaten was actually a healthy supplement that was full of good-for-you vitamins and botanicals that would help you de-stress and even sleep better, you'd be happy and wonder where you could get a bottle of those yummy little treats. A once-a-day gummy that is packed with all the ingredients you need to counteract how stress sabotages your body's systems? Sounds great!

Pills and Gummies Are Not the Answer

Unfortunately, that person is full of it. Our brains know this, which is why we're immediately skeptical when someone starts talking about something that sounds like a load of BS.

But, we also want things to be easy – it's why the supplement and ingestibles category has seen a 133 percent increase in customer demand over the past five years (Boots, 2021). Anxiety, menopause, and hormone balancing have all seen stratospheric rises in search volume, according to recent data compiled by consumer trend agency Spate – 21.5 percent, 32.1 percent, and a staggering 193.8 percent year-over-year growth, respectively (Pitt, 2024).

In theory, supplements seem like exactly the solution to our overstimulated, undernourished, sleep-deprived, tech-addicted lives. After all, the ingredient labels are stuffed with formulations that tout ingredients we've been told are good for us and that our bodies need to be healthy. **But popping a pill or, even worse, chewing a sugary gummy, and expecting it to magically fix what ails us is the very definition of magical thinking.**

Or, perhaps more accurately, it's more in line with pharmaceutical thinking.

Supplements Are Considered Food, So Manufacturers Don't Have to Do Studies to Show Theirs Work

The pharmaceutical industry is big business in the United States – considering it is only one of two countries in the world that allows drug manufacturers to market prescription drugs directly to the public, it's no surprise that Americans have a mentality of fixing whatever ails them with a pill.

Unfortunately, what many people don't realize is that supplements and prescription medication are not formulated or regulated in the same ways. And that's the reason why we have what's probably the most expensive urine in the world – the majority of those pricey supplements you are taking every day aren't actually getting into your system but are just going right down the drain.

That's because **pharmaceuticals are regulated by the Food and Drug Administration (FDA) as drugs, meaning they must be clinically tested and approved by the FDA** *before* **they hit the market, whereas supplements are considered food, meaning the FDA does not require them to be clinically tested for** efficacy and they do not have to be tested by the FDA before going to market.

Instead, the FDA and the Federal Trade Commission monitor brands on a semi-regular basis, typically only removing problematic products after they are already on the market and have demonstrated that they are in violation of what's known as DSHEA, the Dietary Supplement Health and Education Act, which requires manufacturers to self-report any claims of adverse effects (Office of Dietary Supplements, 1994). I'm guessing you can see where problems might arise with this model.

That's not to say that pharmaceuticals are inherently good and safe by any means – take one look at the opioid crisis America is facing. A highly addictive drug that was tested and approved, then prescribed by doctors with a cavalier attitude.

Supplements are not inherently bad because they lack FDA regulation and pharmaceuticals are not inherently good because they have that oversight. There are always outliers in each category and it's important to not make generalizations about either simply due to government oversight.

Supplement Labels Can Be Misleading

While many supplement brands have good intentions and truly want to create quality, safe, efficacious products with scientifically backed formulations, there are others that see the growth potential of the market and do only the bare minimum to be compliant with DSHEA. That's not even counting the, shall I say, unscrupulous few who play the game of "how long can I put this on the shelves and make money until someone catches me" shell game.

There's an infamous *New York Times* story that documented just how misleading many supplement labels can be – in 2015 the New York Attorney General paid a surprise visit to national retailers with a significant presence in the wellness supplement category (O'Connor, 2015). They took top-selling store brand supplements from GNC, Target, Walgreens, and Walmart and tested them to see exactly what was in the bottles.

Not only did they find that the products did not contain the levels of the ingredients listed on the bottle, four out of five of the products didn't even contain *any* of the herbs that were listed on the bottle.

Instead, lab tests found fillers such as powdered rice, asparagus, houseplants(!), and even some ingredients that could be dangerous to those with allergies – none of which were listed anywhere on the ingredient labels of the products. Misleading would be a bit of an understatement here. If you bought a valerian root supplement to help with your sleep issues, only to discover it not only didn't contain any valerian root, but instead was full of powdered radish, houseplants, and wheat (an actual lab result one test found), you'd be pretty upset, especially if you had a wheat allergy.

Why You Can Rely on the Results of Clinical Testing of Rebalance Products

Many brands also like to use the term clinically tested, another phrase that's not currently regulated. And while you would hope that any product making claims about what their supplement can do for you, especially one promising better sleep or cortisol regulation or hormone balancing, the reality is that independent, third-party clinical testing is the exception in the supplement category, not the rule.

**The majority of products that say they have clinically tested ingredients aren't referring to their specific formulation, but rather the thousands of clinical tests that have been done in the past on well-established ingredients, like vitamin C or

vitamin B12. Typically, because independent clinical testing is both expensive and time-consuming, **many brands lack either the funds or the patience to invest in their own testing on their specific formulation that proves that their product has the results that it says it does.**

When we were developing the Rebalance Health products, we knew that science had to take precedence. Because this was a product that was in part created to help my wife support her cortisol fluctuations that were exacerbated by her Cushing's syndrome, I wasn't going to rely on the work of others to prove efficacy or safety. From its unique delivery method to its impact on cortisol levels, Rebalance products are all formulated and clinically tested with the help of an evidence-based team of endocrinologists, hormone experts, naturopaths, and age management physicians.

We conducted what's called an institutional review board (IRB) open-label studies on our products. An IRB is an FDA requirement for human clinical trials that is formally designated to review and monitor biomedical research. They have the power to approve, require modifications in (to secure approval), or block or disapprove research.

The results of our IRB-approved open-label study on the Rebalance Hot Flash System for those experiencing menopause symptoms were so compelling that the North American Menopause Society's *Menopause Journal* (Rebalance Health, Inc., 2024) published the abstract along with preliminary results of the 2023 study, and the *Journal of Nutraceuticals and Food Science* published the complete results of the 2023 study, which **demonstrated a staggering 90 percent reduction of menopausal symptoms in participants, including an 80 percent reduction in hot flashes** (Rebalance Health, Inc., 2025).

For many supplement brands, putting the words "clinically tested" in their marketing materials creates a sense of legitimacy, letting people think that there has been scientific testing done on the products they are purchasing and consuming that proves the claims being made are factual and backed-up by independent research and science. Unfortunately, that's not always the case and the term is not regulated by any government agencies – it's very similar to the word "natural" in the beauty industry. It has no real meaning outside of how brands choose to define it. **Some – like us here at Rebalance Health – do use it the way that you imagine it means, conducting scientific tests with independent agencies to verify the data and research.** But, still others just think that it makes their product sound more legitimate, so will use it to advertise to a more-informed consumer looking for science-backed products.

One thing you can be sure of is that any brand who has invested in the time and money it takes to conduct true independent clinical research will have the studies and the science and data to back up those claims readily accessible on their website or in consumer materials. **The results of our studies were so compelling, we wanted to shout them from the rooftops, which is why we submitted them to multiple professional associations for recognition, in addition to making sure they are available on our website for consumers to look through for themselves. Show, don't tell, if you will.**

Why We Call Rebalance Products for Balancing Cortisol Superceuticals®

When I was speaking with experts, attempting to find the best solution to help positively impact cortisol, I learned quickly that there is no one solution to addressing a cortisol imbalance – **because cortisol affects so many of your body's vital functions, there isn't a** single botanical or vitamin or mineral that can meaningfully impact it in a way that would be impactful to someone dealing with chronic stress.

That's because balancing cortisol is a multi-pronged approach that encompasses everything from managing daily stress to regulating your sleep cycle. It also involves ensuring that the ingredients are able to be absorbed by the body – if an herb is unable to get where it needs to be in the body to do what it does best, there's little chance it will have the intended effect.

With all of this information in mind, it led me to the notion of a Superceutical® – a super-powered nutraceutical where every ingredient serves a specific purpose. Instead of fillers, additives, and preservatives that have no nutritional benefit to the body, each doctor-formulated product contains only ingredients that are evidence-backed, chosen specifically to work synergistically to create a bio-available formulation where every ingredient plays a crucial role in helping the body function optimally and better balance its hormones.

These are just a few of the key ingredients that our team identified as worthy of inclusion into our Superceutical® blends:

Ashwagandha: No doubt an herb you've heard plenty about recently, Ashwagandha has been used in Ayurvedic medicine for thousands of years. It's adaptogenic, meaning it helps your body adapt to what's happening around you, allowing your body to better manage stress. It's known for its ability to help relieve stress (Bhattacharya et al., 1987), increase energy levels, and improve concentration (Choudhary, Bhattacharyya and Bose, 2017). Studies have found that it not only helps calm the brain (Chai et al., 2020), reduce inflammation, lower blood pressure, and boost the immune system, but that it also has a significant impact on improving sleep quality (Deshpande et al., 2020).

Bacopa: Another traditional Ayurvedic remedy, *Bacopa* is a plant that has been used traditionally to address cognitive function and stress responses involving the nervous system. It's a powerful antioxidant that can increase certain brain chemicals that are involved in thinking, memorizing, concentrating, and learning (Calabrese et al., 2008). Some research shows that it may even have the ability to protect the brain cells from chemicals associated with Alzheimer's disease (Simpson, Pase and Stough, 2015). Studies with *Bacopa* have shown both immediate and long-term benefits, with participants reporting an effect of feeling a sense of well-being and calmness with short-term use, while those who continued to take *Bacopa* for a six-to-12-week period showed better results with its beneficial cognitive effects (Peth-Nui et al., 2012).

***Cordyceps* Mushrooms:** The *Cordyceps* mushrooms – once prized by royal families in Tibet and China for its ability to create a tonic that delivered immunity, vitality, energy, and stamina – is once again in-demand for those who understand the power of adaptogenic ingredients (Lin and Li, 2011). Known as an immune system modulator, *Cordyceps* mushrooms help promote overall endocrine system health, supporting the liver and kidneys and communication between the adrenal glands, which are largely responsible for producing the hormones that regulate your stress response (Nagata, Tajima and Uchida, 2006). *Cordyceps* also contain beta-glucan polysaccharides, which have been studied to support the immune system, overall wellness, and healthy cell growth and turnover (Smiderle et al., 2014).

DIM: Diindolylmethane, commonly known as DIM, is a natural compound found in cruciferous vegetables like broccoli, brussel sprouts, and cauliflower. Think of it as a "dimmer" switch for overactive hormones – it works to balance hormones, primarily estrogen and testosterone (Thomson, Ho and Strom, 2016). During menopause (and, to some degree, andropause, the male version of menopause), when the production of these crucial hormones is thrown out of balance due to this natural life stage change, the resulting dip in estrogen and testosterone production can lead to everything from hot flashes to disrupted sleep to low sex drive. Which is why having a compound like DIM in your daily routine can help keep your hormone levels balanced and your systems at their optimal and healthy function.

L-Theanine: A powerful antioxidant and amino acid found in green tea and some mushrooms, L-Theanine is the calming plant you need to help you relax, relieve stress, and induce sleep (Sarris et al., 2018). It can even help improve memory and increase focus. L-Theanine's sleepy time benefits have been shown in multiple studies, which suggest that it works by helping you to relax before bedtime, letting you fall asleep more easily and sleep more deeply (Roa, Ozeki and Juneja, 2015). The theory is that these benefits result from the specific effects that the amino acid has on brain chemicals that play a vital role in sleep (Dasdelen et al., 2022).

L-Tryptophan: Another sleep-inducing amino acid, you've probably heard of L-Tryptophan thanks to the post-Thanksgiving nap that a giant plate of turkey and gravy makes you want to take. But, that's not the only benefit – it also has the ability to uplift your mood. That's because L-Tryptophan can be converted into a molecule called 5-HTP (5-Hydroxytryptophan) which produces serotonin (Birdsall, 1998) and melatonin (Hajak et al., 1991). Serotonin (a.k.a. The Happy Hormone) affects everything from your mood to cognition to sleep, while melatonin is the hormone our body produces in preparation for sleep. Once your body produces serotonin from L-Tryptophan, it can be converted into melatonin, influencing a healthy circadian rhythm and sleep-wake cycle, meaning you'll feel both content and ready for a good night's sleep with this amino acid in your nighttime supplement regimen (Bravo et al., 2012).

Maca: For a plant that looks like the lovechild of a turnip and a potato, this ancient root is not what one would consider a sexy food. But Maca is a proven aphrodisiac that also functions as an adaptogen to help enhance both memory and athletic performance. Studies have shown that Maca can be an effective treatment for those dealing with decreased sexual desire – either due to hormone imbalance (Gonzales et al., 2002) or antidepressant-induced (Dording et al., 2015). Studies have also demonstrated its benefits as a treatment for age-related cognitive decline, helping to slow down the process and improving existing cognitive function (Guo, 2016).

Magnolia Bark: A standout plant in traditional Chinese medicine, Magnolia bark is the supplement equivalent of a comforting hug. Filled with bioactive compounds that function as anti-inflammatory, anti-bacterial, and anti-allergic agents, Magnolia bark can help calm, soothe, and de-stress (Kalman et al., 2008). It also works as an anxiolytic (Woodbury et al., 2013), helping to lower anxiety and depression, as well as a natural sedative by assisting in GABA production, quieting excitatory neurons and directly helping to promote sleep (Chen et al., 2012). Magnolia bark is a natural sleep aid that helps calm an overactive brain, making it easier for you to drift off into dreamland and regenerate and prepare for the following day. Research has also shown that it can help maintain acetylcholine, a neurotransmitter that helps the brain process memory and learning.

Melatonin: One of the most popular supplements on the market, melatonin is unique because it is a hormone that your body naturally produces, but it's also one of the most misunderstood ingredients in the wellness category (Zisapel, 2018). Many people still believe that they need to take a melatonin product at bedtime, when the reality of this hormone is that our body releases it as a signal that it's time to start getting ready to wind down and prepare for bed. Melatonin plays a key role in your circadian rhythm, increasing when it starts to get dark outside and thus signaling to your body it's time for sleep (Auld et al., 2016). It also binds to receptors in the body helping you relax. It's not an ingredient you take to put you to sleep, but rather one you take to prepare your body to induce sleep – it regulates your sleep-wake cycle and ensures you stay within your natural bedtime schedule, which, in turn, helps keep your cortisol levels balanced (because you are getting deep, restful sleep at the optimal times). Melatonin has also been shown to stimulate the release of HGH (human growth hormone), a hormone that plays an important role in body composition, cell repair, and growth (Nassar et al., 2007). It also boosts muscle growth, body strength, and exercise performance.

Oat Straw: Taken from the stems and leaves of the unripe *Avena sativa* (a.k.a. oat) plant, oat straw is a nourishing extract that is rich in vitamins and minerals such as calcium, iron, and magnesium. It's known to have a soothing effect and can be a restorative herb for those that feel depleted, tired, and cold, or for the person who feels constantly burnt out and can't function without their daily hit of coffee (Kennedy et al., 2020).

Reishi Mushroom: Often referred to as the "Mushroom of Immortality," Reishi mushroom has been prized in traditional Chinese medicine for centuries for its longevity and overall health benefits. As an adaptogenic plant, Reishi can help support the immune system, aid in liver function, improve cognitive ability, reduce stress, and lessen fatigue (Tang et al., 2005). It's also been shown to help improve sleep quality by supporting the adrenal glands while you slumber, allowing you to feel recharged and get good, quality sleep without feeling drowsy the next morning (Liao et al., 2018).

Now, you might be thinking that some, if not all of these ingredients sound familiar. It's possible you've not only heard of, but maybe even already take some of these herbs and plants as supplements already. Which wouldn't be surprising – they are all extremely well researched and tested, trusted by doctors and scientists. That's why my team and I chose them to be a part of the Rebalance system.

But, what makes a product effective is about more than just what's in it. You can have the best ingredients on the planet in your formula, but if they aren't getting into the body where they need to go (and, at the right time), they aren't going to have an impact.

The goal of any supplement, as Dr. Dorfman points out, is about putting your body back into what's called homeostasis – that's a state of balance within the body where all of your internal functions are operating optimally. Nothing is hitting an extreme, be it overactive or underproductive.

Too often we identify a singular issue and focus on that problem, looking for something to fix it. That's a pharmaceutical approach – take this pill to fix this symptom.

What we should be doing instead is looking at our bodies as a whole system. For instance, you can't separate sleep from a cortisol imbalance, so if you're trying to solve one without addressing the other, you're setting yourself up for failure. **You need to look at the bigger picture and address the whole body, not seek out a singular ingredient for a singular problem. And, you need to make sure that the formulation is getting into your system in the first place.**

Most Pill and Gummy Ingredients Are Destroyed in the Digestive System

Traditional pill-based supplements are not designed with efficacy in mind – they are made to be efficient and to encourage compliance. They want you to continue taking them on a regular basis, and you are more likely to do that if it's a simple pill you take once a day. Quick, easy, efficient.

Unfortunately, your digestive system doesn't work like that. When anything is swallowed, it travels through your digestive system and into the gut. During that journey, it encounters digestive acids and enzymes that function to break down food, help absorb nutrients, and "expel" everything else as waste.

From your saliva to your intestines to your liver, everything is working together to break down food into nourishment and energy. Those acids and enzymes don't discriminate between a giant, chewy steak and a delicate little pill – it's like a trash compactor. **Your stomach isn't analyzing what's going through and treating different things with gentler levels of digestive acids than others.**

It's for this reason that most pills contain a durable coating on the outside. That's to protect the ingredients as they travel through the digestive system so that they aren't immediately destroyed before the nutrients can get where they need to be. Unfortunately, it's not a very effective system. **The majority of those ingredients are still getting destroyed by the gut before they can impact your system in a meaningful way.**

Some brands have introduced gummies as an alternative option for those that don't like to or are unable to swallow pills, but they offer even less consistency as gummies are extremely difficult to control potency and stability of ingredients in their formulations. Not to mention, many gummies can be packed with as much as two to eight grams of sugar per serving (UCLA Health, 2022).

We knew there had to be a better delivery system, so we conducted extensive research into the best ways to ensure the body gets the vitamins and minerals it needs. We came across research that showed zinc lozenges were a more effective form of fighting the common cold than zinc tablets or gummies – because the zinc is carried through blood vessels in the lining of the mouth, rather than having to travel through the digestive system first, scientists believe the mineral was more effectively delivered to the body (Eby, Davis and Halcomb, 1984). In fact, after IVs or injection, lozenges and nasal sprays are considered the next best delivery method.

It's because of this research and input from doctors and scientists that we decided to make the Rebalance Health Systems a lozenge delivery to ensure those beneficial herbs and botanicals had the highest probability of getting absorbed.

To Support the Body's Natural Rhythms, We Created a Line of Lozenges for Daytime and Evening

After we had perfected the ingredients and the delivery system, there was one more key factor that we needed to address in order to ensure that Rebalance Health System was truly a change maker. While convenience is nice in theory, the idea that taking one pill a day can address the multitude of system functions that you are trying to bring back into balance is wishful thinking.

There are some ingredients that promote restfulness and relaxation, while others promote energy and concentration. Those are two diametrically opposed actions. You don't want to be energized and focused at bedtime and you don't want to be relaxed and prepared for restful sleep in the morning.

So, instead of trying to combine all of those ingredients in one lozenge, we knew we needed to create different products for day and night tailored to the body's natural rhythms. Each one has its own specific blend of herbs and botanicals to support the key systems and functions that need balancing for that time of day.

Not only does this ensure that you are getting what you need, when you need it, but it also ensures that you are maintaining significant levels of each throughout the day.

Our bodies process nutrients on a consistent cycle, both in our sleeping and waking hours. There is no level of nutrients that can be crammed into a once-a-day pill that would carry you through an entire 24-hour cycle and be retained in the body at a functioning level throughout the day to help you achieve a meaningful impact on your stress levels and sleep quality.

Even many prescription medications like antibiotics require multiple doses to be most effective; likewise pain medication and cold and flu medication all require multiple doses to be effective.

We've just become so obsessed with convenience that we've thrown true efficacy out the window – something is better than nothing, seems to be the dominant school of thought. But, when it comes to chronic stress and sleep deficiencies, that just won't cut it. The impacts on our health are too critical and too wide ranging to sit back and say that we'll settle for half measures.

You Have to Do Your Part, Too

One key thing that many people forget is what a supplement actually is – but it's right there in the name. A supplement is meant to supplement a healthy diet and lifestyle, not replace it.

Someone who takes a scientifically proven and tested system like Rebalance Health but doesn't make any adjustments to their diet, exercise, or lifestyle and continues to practice unhealthy habits will continue to have health issues.

"You can't just take one product and not do anything else and expect it to be beneficial," explains Dr. Dorfman. "This is one of the tools in the toolkit that you will use to help with sleep, stress, and cortisol levels. It's a multi-pronged approach."

And, part of that approach involves finding ways to minimize your daily reliance and interactions with your devices, in addition to adding more daily practices to your routine that are scientifically proven to help lower cortisol, build better relationships, improve intimacy, and get better quality sleep.

Chapter 10
JOMO Is the New FOMO: Outsmarting Burnout, Brain Fog & Bad Habits

There is no enemy to the peaceful solitude of a quiet afternoon with a good book, or a fun date night out with your partner, quite like the group text. The steadily escalating cacophony of buzzes or dings as one person on the text chain chimes in, and another sends a gif, and yet another responds with an emoji, and still another reacts to a previous text from minutes before can send even the most patient person into a fit of rage, ready to throw their phone out the window to get some peace from the never-ending alerts. It's the agony and ecstasy of being in the loop with your friend group – held at the mercy of whoever decided to drop a random thought into the chain or bring a zombie thread roaring back to life after a relatively peaceful period of digital quietude.

On the one hand, it's nice to be connected with your friend group and know the ins and outs of everyone's lives or what they're finding interesting in any given moment. On the other, it can be extremely distracting (to put it mildly) to have your phone blow up with text after text when you're consciously trying to be present in your actual life. Knowing what we know about the distractive nature of push alerts and the mere presence of our phones, it's hard enough to actively disengage from invasive technology, but add in a symphony of notifications repeatedly blasting through the quiet as you're just trying to protect your peace and it can be nigh on impossible to carve out that precious time away from your devices.

Then, of course, there's this burdensome sense of needing to know everything going on in the world in order to keep up with a conversation. Whenever anything remotely newsworthy happens, there's always that one friend who jumps into the thread with commentary or questions for the group.

If you're someone who is actively trying to cut back on the amount of time you spend online, or just trying to limit your news intake for your own mental well-being, it can be frustrating for the conversation to shift and you to be unable to follow its trajectory, forcing you to either admit your ignorance or quickly start Googling to find out what everyone is talking about.

Whether it's pop culture or current events, there's a certain anxiety tied to being the person in the group chat who's out of the loop and brings the conversation to a screeching halt because you either don't know who everyone is talking about or have no idea what event they are referring to.

It's the digital version of FOMO – fear of missing out. You don't want to be the reason everyone starts another group chat without you, leaving you to slowly be left behind or wondering why the formerly active text thread has suddenly gone silent.

The New FOMO Isn't About Missing the Party – It's About Staying on Top of the Info You Need to Make Your Friends Laugh

In the early aughts, FOMO was coined as a direct response to social media and the fabulous lives it seemed everyone was living based on what was posted online (Gupta and Sharma, 2021). Often what people forgot was that our online selves were carefully curated, only showing our most exciting moments and adventures – very few were posting the mundane activities that made up their everyday existence.

FOMO was what caused us to be apprehensive that we were missing out on unique experiences that those in our social networks had access to. That we were somehow socially inferior if we did not also engage in all those Instagrammable parties and trips and experiences. It caused us to go to great lengths to showcase only the most picture-perfect parts of our lives while simultaneously being hyper-focused on what everyone else was doing and wondering why we weren't also either invited to the same parties and events or living the same kind of lifestyle.

FOMO, as silly as it sounds, is something psychologists attribute to causing real-world harm, creating a problematic type of attachment to social media that can lead to lack of sleep, emotional tension, negative effects on physical well-being, anxiety, and a lack of emotional control (Altuwairiqi, Jiang and Ali, 2019).

While we've wised up exponentially since those naive early days when we believed everything we saw on social media was an accurate representation of someone's daily life, that doesn't mean FOMO no longer exists – it's simply evolved into something more nuanced.

Instead of worrying we're missing out on rewarding experiences that others are having without us, which in turn leaves us with unmet social needs, we're now worried about missing out on information that would help us create social connections with our existing group of friends or new acquaintances. The loneliness epidemic has left us desperate for connections and eager to be good conversation partners, but with that comes an anxiety of being out of the loop – of not being able to connect with someone about a topic because we missed a crucial piece of information within the endless stream of content we're being bombarded with every second of the day.

Did you read what Taylor Swift posted about her (maybe, possibly, hopefully) new album? Do you agree with that *The Cut* article on modern etiquette? (The Cut, 2023). Did you hear the latest episode of *Fresh Air*? Did you see that *Saturday Night Live* cold open? What did you think about that awards show acceptance speech? Can you believe what just happened in the news? Isn't [insert hit show/movie/podcast/book/album/TikToker] the best?

If someone brings up any of those topics and you aren't up-to-date with them, to answer them honestly with an "oh, I'm actually unfamiliar with that," can typically lead to a trailing off in the conversation.

As we try to find ways to connect with each other, content of all types has increasingly become a way to bond with others. We spend so much of our free time looking at screens that it's only natural that many of us are consuming the same content on those screens and would use that as a way to bond.

But, what's getting lost in that sea of videos, episodes, articles, tweets, and posts is that it's also creating pressure to consume that content in order to stay informed – it's like adult homework. If you're not in the know, you risk getting left behind by your peers. We have information FOMO, but the joke is that there's only so much content you can actually watch, listen to, or read on any given day. No matter how chronically online you are, there's always going to be something you miss.

And – brace yourself for this – that's ok. **You don't want to be someone who sees every piece of content. Being perpetually attached to a device in an attempt to be in the loop so you can better connect with others will leave you constantly staring at a screen and missing out on what's going on around you.**

There are other ways to connect with people that don't involve talking about content. Hobbies – remember those? – and shared life experiences can be a great jumping off point for conversation starters.

How to Replace FOMO with JOMO – the Joy of Missing Out – and Reclaim Your Peace, Happiness, and Real-life Relationships

Perhaps that's why the concept of JOMO – the joy of missing out – has started to catch on as people realize that constantly staring at a screen in an effort to stay in the loop is causing them to miss out on the important moments in their life (https://www.psychologytoday.com/us/blog/happiness-is-state-mind/201807/jomo-the-joy-missing-out).

JOMO is the rejection of the addictive nature of technology, replacing the quick dopamine hits that social media likes fire off in our brains for the more lasting mental health benefits of being present in your life and the environment and people around you.

Rather than chasing that feel-good dopamine surge that happens when we spend time on social media – a short-lived burst that fades quickly and requires you to stay immersed in your screen, scrolling endlessly to keep the sensation coming – **JOMO is about slowing down and appreciating what's in front of you. It means being intentional with your time to schedule things that are truly important to you, rather than getting sucked into wasting time in a scroll hole, consuming content online for hours or lurking on your connections' social media feeds to see what everyone is doing without you.**

Doing something with intention, be it finding time in your day to work out or scheduling time to meet a friend for a catch-up session at your favorite restaurant, prioritizes not only your time, but your health and relationships. And it allows you to do those things consciously and decisively, rather than letting a computer algorithm passively lead you toward the next thing you view.

By taking the time to focus on yourself and the things you actually want to do or accomplish, rather than being steered by technology, you discover a greater understanding of who you are as a person and what your skills and interests truly are. **JOMO also allows you to be present in a moment, rather then have anxiety around what it is you are missing or what it is you should be doing.** If you are constantly chasing the digital zeitgeist, you are always playing catch-up and will never have time to embrace and enjoy experiences as they happen.

Too often when we attend an event or travel somewhere, we feel the urge to document it with our phones – from concerts to meals to picturesque spots in nature. We've lost the ability to simply exist in a moment in time and enjoy it for what it is. Viewing life through a screen doesn't have the same effect on your mind and body as being fully present in that moment.

There's also a slowness and stillness that comes from disconnecting from our devices in order to focus more on our real-world lives. **Technology and FOMO, with their very nature, create a false sense of urgency – everything must be done quickly or you miss out on the novelty.** No one wants to be the person who sends a meme that everyone has seen a million times already. If you're not first, you're last.

FOMO also pushes us to prioritize efficiency and multitasking, constantly striving to be better and work harder, even in our leisure time. Why concentrate on one thing when you can be doing three? It's how the whole concept of the side hustle turned what was supposed to be our enjoyable hobbies into money-making businesses. If you're not capitalizing on your free time, then you're wasting it.

But, that's not how the human body works. We are not machines created to monetize every aspect of our lives. We do not need to be in constant competition with our peers to be the most enterprising individual of our generation. It's ok to like knitting and not open up an Etsy shop to sell your creations. Or to write for the love of writing and not to become the next bestselling author. Or to decorate intricate cupcakes and not turn them into super-popular TikTok videos. Some things can be just for you to enjoy as a hobby that fulfills you or relaxes you.

Another perk of JOMO? When we are more intentional with our time, we not only find the time to do things we enjoy, it's also easier to find the motivation to be better to ourselves. One of the hardest parts about eating healthier and exercising regularly is finding the motivation to get into a regular routine. But healthy eating and daily exercise are good for our bodies and for keeping our cortisol in balance.

And, while everyone wants there to be some secret hack to lower cortisol through a niche diet or special exercise routine, the simple answer is that the real solution is to go to bed at the same time every night, obtain seven to eight hours of uninterrupted sleep every night, eat a nutritious and balanced diet, and make time for at least 60 minutes a day of low-to moderate-intensity cardio and weight-bearing exercises.

To Heal Your Relationship with Food and Stress, Fix What You Eat – and When You Eat – Because That Will Reduce How Much You Eat

Anyone who lived through the 1990s can remember very distinctly the shift that happened when marketers realized there was big business in healthy living. People began to want to treat their bodies better by eating well. Unfortunately, we weren't as informed as we are now and so-called "diet culture" took hold. Instead of focusing on whole foods and healthy fruits and vegetables, the focus became about restricting calories and "low-fat" foods.

It seemed every time you turned on the TV, there was a new kind of fad diet to follow that promised to slim your waistline and burn belly fat. There was a slightly hilarious moment (we have to laugh to keep from crying) when everything was put in a green packaging in an attempt to trick us into thinking we were eating something that was good for us, when in reality it was usually 100 percent processed food with little to no nutritional value. Sorry Snackwell's, but you weren't fooling anybody with those cookies – at least not for long, anyways.

And yet, even after that collective nutritional fever dream, so many people are still chasing shortcuts, despite knowing that the only true path to living and aging well is to eat a consistently healthy diet full of whole, unprocessed foods and to get regular exercise that's a mix of cardio and strength training. We've been taught this since middle school health class, it's been backed up by study after study, and yet, when someone comes along with a pill or a "hack" to optimize our metabolism, our ears can't help but perk up. Surely there has to be an easier way, right?

The fundamental problem with this way of thinking is that people, despite talking about wanting to live healthier, are often still stuck in this diet culture mindset. And while that's harmful for our self-esteem and well-being for myriad reasons, it also does absolutely nothing for our overall goal of better sleep and more balanced cortisol. Diet culture thrives on the idea of weight loss over all else – the goal, no matter the fad, is to lose weight. But losing weight doesn't necessarily help create healthier habits. It can create a type of disordered eating that shifts the focus on restriction and deprivation, rather than focusing on changing our relationship with food.

For someone looking to have a healthier relationship with food and stress, the goal is not how much you eat, but rather what you eat and when you eat it.

When you are stressed out, you tend to consume foods that are either extremely easy and efficient to eat in a fast-paced environment or you turn to foods that comfort you and make you feel better (Dakanalis et al., 2023). Both of these situations usually lead to people consuming foods that are highly processed and low in nutritional value. It can also lead to more snacking and eating late, as well as associating sugary, fatty foods as a reward or a mood stabilizer.

The reality is that eating late and eating high-fat, processed, sugary foods is a one-way ticket to disrupting your sleep cycle, leaving you with cortisol levels that are too high and skyrocketing stress that will have you turning to food as a coping mechanism, repeating the cycle all over again the next day. Food is not and should not be a stress deterrent – no matter how many little treats you convince yourself you deserve after a stressful day, loading up on junk food and plopping on the couch to scroll through your social media after a particularly terrible day at work or a fight with your partner is going to have the exact opposite effect on your cortisol.

Instead, food should be considered your fuel – an essential you need to power up your body and get you through your day. Instead of jumping from fad diet to fad diet (or, rather, viral TikTok hack), look for lean proteins, fresh fruits and veggies, whole grains, plenty of hydration, omega fatty acids, adaptogenic herbs, and the essential vitamins and minerals your mind and body need to fuel your daily activities and get the best possible sleep.

That combination will vary for everyone because every person is different – a postmenopausal woman and a 25-year-old man are not going to need the same fuel because their bodies are fundamentally different. Even people within the same demographic may have different dietary needs, simply because we all operate differently. Some people exercise more, some less. Some have certain vitamin and mineral deficiencies, others don't. Some people have genetic predispositions to conditions like osteoporosis, some don't.

Finding the right mix of foods that work for you means knowing what your body needs to operate at its peak. Consulting with your physician is a great place to start to learn if you are deficient in any essential vitamins and minerals and learn what foods to add to your diet to make up for them.

The Foundation of Your Well-being Is Healthy Habits

While products like the Rebalance Health Systems can help provide a supplement to a healthy diet and lifestyle, it can't replace one. If you are constantly stress eating trash foods into the wee hours of the morning while firmly planted on the couch, phone in hand, your sleep will suffer and your cortisol will spike.

But, if you supplement a healthy diet with Rebalance, while making sure to eat early, go to bed before that cortisol dip at 11 p.m., and disconnect from your devices well before bedtime, then you'll see the benefits with more energy, better sleep quality, and less overall stress.

It's always amusing to me when a healthy habit I've been following for decades suddenly becomes a "trend" on social media. The latest example is the viral TikTok health trend of the 30-30-30 method. It consists of eating 30 grams of protein within 30 minutes of waking up and then doing 30 minutes of low-intensity cardio exercise. While there are no studies to back this trend up, the idea that fitness influencers have been pedaling is that it "jump-starts" your metabolism, making it easier to lose weight. See, there's that diet culture again.

For me, the idea of eating a protein-rich breakfast when I wake up and exercising early in the morning is not about weight loss – it's about ensuring my body doesn't eat my muscle I'm working so hard to build, not to mention ensuring my cortisol stays balanced and I'm in the best possible mood for whatever the day may bring. Because, **just like sleep, exercise is a universally beneficial activity; however, it still matters when you do it.**

Morning Is Best – But the Right Time to Exercise Is When You'll Actually Do It

Studies have found that exercising late at night can have an impact on the quality of your sleep. That's because exercise initially causes a rise in cortisol concentrations – not exactly something you want at 10 p.m. (Haupt et al., 2021). Ideally, cortisol would go back to its normal levels after exercise, but because the majority of us are in constant states of high stress, exercise can exacerbate that stress if you don't give your body time to recover. That means proper stretching, hydration, and taking time to wind down after a workout, which is difficult to do late at night. It could also cause your cortisol levels to deviate from their natural circadian rhythms – spiking late at night when they should be hitting their lowest point.

If you exercise in the morning, when cortisol is at its peak, you are taking advantage of when your body and mind are at their most alert to get a boost in your workout. You're also ensuring that you are aligning your morning cortisol surge with the cortisol surge that occurs alongside a workout.

Exercise releases cortisol, resulting in a drop in cortisol levels post – session. This creates a calm, relaxed feeling after your workout and helps you start your day with a clear-eyed focus and feeling that will make the rest of your day easier to manage, especially if you've got a relatively stressful schedule ahead of you.

And, if you're feeling extra stressed, some experts even say that it's best to dial down the intensity of your workout so that you aren't releasing as much cortisol during your workouts and overloading your system (Kassel, 2024). So, if you're going through a stressful time at work or in a relationship, try dialing down the intensity of your workout or workout less often for a few weeks to help give your body a break from the deluge of cortisol that's flooding your body.

Now, to be clear, any exercise is better than no exercise. If you have the kind of schedule that doesn't allow you the time to sneak in 60 minutes to workout in the morning, then exercise when you can, even if that means it's at night. Just try not to make your nighttime workout a high-intensity HIIT session or a two-hour endurance run that leaves you gasping on the floor. Instead, try a lower-intensity weight training or yoga practice or do those high-intensity workouts less often or at 70 to 85 percent of your usual capacity. **And, definitely don't sacrifice your necessary seven to eight hours of sleep in order to wake up early to work out – you need that full night's rest to keep your cortisol in balance, so giving that up in order to squeeze in an early workout negates the benefits.**

But, don't use your inability to do a morning workout as an excuse to not work out at all just because it's not the optimal time. It's akin to eating one french fry and thinking that you've messed up your whole healthy eating plan for the day, so you might as well eat the rest of that large fries and add some chicken tenders, a milkshake, and some cookies to your order.

Self-sabotaging because you can't find perfection only leads to a downward spiral of unhealthy habits which serve to exacerbate your stress.

While it might feel good in the short term to sleep in late, stress-eat comfort foods, and veg on the couch, the long-term effects on your health will only serve to create a cascade of problems that will in turn contribute to chronic stress and higher cortisol.

There's always that little voice in the back of your head telling you that you should be doing something differently when you are acting unhealthy – nobody likes that voice because it's a bit of a know-it-all, but it's right. The best way to shut that voice down is not to ignore it, but to listen to it and start making those beneficial changes to your routine.

Start Small with Reducing Screen Time – Make Your Bedroom a No-device Zone

Finding ways to limit your screen time is one of the most important of those necessary changes you can make to benefit your cortisol levels – and one of the most difficult. But it can pay the most dividends in the form of better sleep, less stress, more focus, and deeper intimacy if you can find ways to detach yourself from the device that's in your hands so often it might as well be another appendage.

As brands find more ways to insert technology into our lives – glasses linked to Google and your social media accounts, those goofy looking Apple goggles that basically turn your eyes into a computer screen – it's becoming more and more difficult to disconnect.

Silicon Valley knows that we know all the screen time isn't great for us, so they keep developing more intrusive ways to keep us connected under the guise of innovation. From TV-sized monitors in our cars (talk about distracted driving) to incorporating AR, VR, and AI into more and more devices, **the goal isn't to make your life easier, but to keep you on your screens for longer – no matter where those screens may be.**

Smartphones, by their very nature, are addictive. You aren't supposed to want to take extended breaks from them. That's the whole point of push notifications, after all. So you have to view your device not as a helpful tool, but as a habit that you need to break.

Going cold turkey is not going to be realistic or, frankly, possible for most people, especially considering that 75 percent of US households don't have landlines and rely on cell phones as their primary form of communication (Blumberg, Luke and National Center for Health Statistics, 2024). Some people even depend on their phones for internet access – a recent survey found that 15 percent of US adults don't have broadband internet access at home and use their smartphones as their primary means of accessing the internet (Gelles-Watnick, 2024). It's a little difficult to cut back on your screen time if the only screen that has internet access is your phone. You might be trying to do a work-related task and suddenly you're distracted by 20 other things that are popping up on your screen.

Rather than try to dramatically cut down on the amount you use your device all at once, try scaling back your usage incrementally.

The first, and most important, step you can take is to remove your phone from your bedroom. Place your charger in an adjacent room if you are worried about missing an important call, but keep your bedroom as a no-device zone. That means all screens – tablets, TVs, smartwatches, video game consoles.

This will help protect your sleep and ensure you aren't getting exposure to blue light that could interfere with the release of melatonin, not to mention electromagnetic fields (EMF). The World Health

Organization and International Agency for Research on Cancer has designated EMFs as possibly carcinogenic to humans, meaning a causal association is considered credible; however further research is needed to establish a link between long-term cell phone usage and brain cancer risk (National Cancer Institute, 2022).

Making your bedroom a no-device zone will also help prevent your exposure to potentially stressful news or interactions with colleagues or loved ones that could spike your cortisol when you should be winding down for the night.

Once you've mastered that all-important nocturnal shift, work your way up to eliminating other technology bad habits.

To Improve Your Focus, Stick to One Screen at a Time

Media multitasking is an all too common occurrence that many of us don't even realize we're doing for the most part. If you're looking at one screen, make sure your focus is on that screen and you aren't dividing your time and attention between multiple devices.

Watch TV without your phone in hand so you can immerse yourself in the story in front of you and retain the information that is unfolding. If you are only half-watching a show while you scroll through Instagram and text with friends, what's the purpose of watching TV in the first place?

While working, your attention should be on the task at hand, not toggling between distractions on your phone and the presentation on which you should be putting the finishing touches for your boss to review. When we get distracted mid-task, our thoughts become disjointed and whatever we were working on is less likely to be our best representation of our skills and knowledge.

Again, if you are having difficulty resisting the phone, place it in another room (or, if you are at the office, put your phone in the desk while you work so it's out of sight and, hopefully, out of mind).

To Improve Your Relationships, Put the Phone out of Sight and out of Reach

When you're with family, friends, or your partner, make a rule for yourself to keep your phone in your purse or pocket so there's less temptation to look at it while you are spending quality real-world time with your loved ones.

You can also go the extra mile and explain to your friends how important offline time is to you and that you want to make a concerted effort to not look at screens when you gather together. Perhaps you institute a "leave your phone by the door" policy when you are at each other's homes. Or make a pact that the first person to pull out their phone at dinner has to pay for a round of drinks.

Extend that same energy into your home by making sure that time spent with your family is time actually spent together. Dinner time means devices are stored in another room and everyone takes time to talk about their day.

If you have young children, resist the temptation to keep them quiet with screens and instead find ways to work around tantrums that don't involve plopping them in front of a tablet with a cartoon on.

For young adults and teenagers, check in with them regularly to understand their social media activity and make sure that they feel comfortable having an honest and open dialogue with you.

Take time with your partner to really listen and focus on building intimacy through touch and re-building the foundations of your relationship. Date each other again, making sure to keep the phones away and to focus on each other's needs, desires, and dreams.

This last part might be the hardest, as we tend to fall into patterns with our loved ones. When our kids are acting out, it's easier to just let them retreat into their comfortable spaces online. When things are tense with our partner, we don't really want to have the difficult conversations – we'd rather angrily tap away at our phones and ignore each other than get in yet another fight.

It's so much easier to send a quick text or DM to a friend to check in than to make the effort to meet up in person. We're busy people, after all, with busy lives.

But, we're also lonely, detached, distracted, and chronically stressed people that need to connect with each other on a deeper level for our own mental and physical health. And technology – with all its dings, and buzzes, and engagement, and conversions – does not allow us the mental space to form and foster those connections.

So, in order to build and nurture our relationships, to protect our sleep, to ensure we can focus on the tasks at hand, and to help regulate our cortisol levels to a more natural ebb and flow, we need to put the devices aside and carve out time without the intrusion of technology.

The Compounding Benefit of Reclaiming Three Hours a Day? A Whole New Life.

The upside of making these necessary shifts is what you'll discover you can do with that free time. Even if you cut your screen time in half, that's still just over three hours a day you're getting back. That's a lot of time to devote back to yourself and your well-being.

In addition to eating better and getting the daily exercise your body needs, you can replace that device time with healthier habits that can also help manage stress and keep your cortisol balanced.

Instead of waking up and immediately grabbing your phone to stare at the blue glow of your screen for an hour,

head outside into the sunshine with your a.m. beverage of choice. Sunshine in the morning has been shown in studies to help regulate your circadian rhythm and lower cortisol levels, making it easier to fall asleep and keep your stress levels in check (Jung et al., 2010). If you have the time or access, go for a hike or walk in the woods to enjoy exposure to nature, another stress-relieving technique that doubles as a great way to get in your daily exercise.

Mindfulness techniques like meditation can help you reconnect with your body and focus on the present, making it a fantastic practice for stress reduction and even as a form of cognitive behavioral therapy (CBT) for depression and anxiety (American Psychological Association, 2019).

Recent studies have also shown the practice of gratitude has proven benefits of helping to lower cortisol and stress levels (McCraty et al., 1998), while also improving sleep quality (Wood et al., 2008). Gratitude journaling, where you focus on positive aspects of your life by writing down the things you are thankful for or appreciate in your life, is an easy way to practice gratitude daily and receive those positive impacts to your mental health and physical well-being.

Making an effort to reconnect with friends and spend actual quality time with your loved ones might be a little trickier as that involves coordination on multiple people's ends, but it's well worth the effort. Once you're no longer scrolling through your friends' social media feeds to stay up-to-date on what's going on in their lives, you'll find you need to be more proactive to stay connected.

If you can't find a way to meet in person more frequently to fulfill those intimacy needs and help prevent loneliness from taking hold, at least make an effort to switch out some of those epic text message interactions for phone calls. It might remind you both how much you miss catching up in person and encourage you to set something up.

Another benefit of cutting back on your time spent with your tech is that you might also find it's easier to schedule time for things that you enjoy, like reading that book you've been meaning to start for the past few months, getting closer to nature with hikes or spending the afternoon gardening, or even getting back into that obscure hobby that you used to enjoy.

What may have seemed insurmountable when you found yourself sucked into the tantalizing allure of your screen for hours on end, is suddenly possible when you make a concerted effort to limit your time on your devices and instead focus on your happiness and health.

Conclusion

From Screen Zombie to Real-Life Rockstar What Actually Works (and What to Ignore Forever)

As I demonstrated at the start of this book, even the motivation of a fictional bargain with a mysterious billionaire reveals just how difficult it can be to completely abandon your device.

Technology has become so intertwined with our daily lives that untangling every facet that we've linked to it over the past two decades can feel like an insurmountable task. From banking to dating to entertainment, we rely on our devices to manage our lives for us.

Many of us have forgotten what life was like before we had a computer in our pocket. Skills like being able to navigate without having a map at our fingertips, our friends' and family's phone numbers, simple math to figure out a tip on our dinner bill without needing to surreptitiously tap it into the calculator, carrying on a conversation without using our devices as a social crutch all seem basic enough, but there is a not-so-insignificant portion of the population who are simply unable to be in a social setting without reaching for their phone as an almost form of emotional support technology.

If there's a lull in the conversation or the connection isn't happening as easily as you had hoped, there's a type of comfort knowing that you can grab your phone and "check out" from an uncomfortable situation by feigning a work or familial obligation that you have to attend to on your phone.

Or, if you're angry with your partner, rather than dealing with the situation – knowing that it will be difficult and uncomfortable – you can sit in angry silence, tapping away at your phone to anonymously ask millions of Redditors if you are overreacting to the situation instead of just talking it out with your significant other.

Yet, as bad as we are at socializing, we're even worse at self-reflection. We've somehow become very good at being alone, yet unable to be alone (and comfortable) with our thoughts.

For the amount of time we spend on our own, most people don't utilize that solitary time to practice positive mental health practices like meditation or gratitude or even just taking the time to look inwardly and reflect on how certain situations or people we encountered during our day impacted us and how we want to move forward from those interactions or feelings. Instead, we bury ourselves in our screens and scroll on, letting the glow comfort us and numb our brains from having to fully feel our range of emotions and dig into why something impacted us the way it did.

Parenting has become similarly fraught, with adults stretched thin and with limited patience for the outbursts that are extremely normal and common with young children. We've been convinced that kids need to be entertained and engaged at every moment and if they are not quiet and acting appropriately then we must manage that – and what better way to manage than by occupying their tiny minds with a screen?

But part of normal childhood development is the ability for kids to create their own forms of entertainment and to nurture budding creativity. Staring at a screen doesn't allow much space for the type of freeform play that lets kids' imaginations run wild. When we occupy every moment and are constantly guiding and creating structured activities for children, we think we are providing safety and stability for them. The reality is we are leaving very little room for the type of free, imaginative play that allows children to learn how to become more independent and naturally develop social skills with their peers.

There's a certain sense of 1990s and Y2K nostalgia that has collectively begun to take hold – both for the generations who experienced it the first time around and those who weren't alive but still feel a magnetic pull for the time period.

From fashion to music to pop culture, the 1990s and early aughts represent a less complicated, more connected time. And, while that's a romanticized view of history (as humans are often prone to doing), it is interesting to see a collective longing for an era when our time was more freely our own and we spent it interacting with each other or devoting it to activities that we enjoyed.

The idea of losing hours just staring at a screen while not actually accomplishing anything is a thoroughly twenty-first century invention – it's not as if screens didn't exist in the 1990s. There was always a limit to the time we could invest in devices, either because of lack of access or lack of technological progress as to what those screens could do. Now, you can spend as much time staring at your phone as you can biologically keep yourself awake. There's no worries about dial-up connection, overheating desktops, or running out of content to consume.

The result is what you've read in this book – we're sitting longer, interacting less, having worse quality sleep, dealing with more mental health challenges, and experiencing chronic stress and worse overall health. But, the solution isn't an extreme swing toward a technology-free life.

As tempting as going off the grid sounds, it's unrealistic for the majority of the population. Instead, focus on an approach to technology that emphasizes balance by doing what the tech companies should have done when they introduced smartphones, social media, and AI the first time around – a responsible attitude toward technology.

Honestly, the only way you could probably get most people to completely give up their devices would be a multi-million-dollar bribe, and even then, it's doubtful most would have the willpower to resist the siren song of their smartphone's push notifications. Which is not a moral failing by any means – entrepreneurs and developers have found ways to make our phones so addictive that their mere presence is enough to distract us.

Here Are Your Reminders of All the Ways Managing Your Cortisol by Cutting Back on Your Technology Use Can Make You Feel Like a Million Bucks (Even If You Wouldn't Take a Million to Give It Up)

So, what does a responsible attitude toward technology look like?

It means self-regulating and installing limits – both on the amount of time you spend on your device and identifying the appropriate times at which to use it. **Find ways to not only cut back on how often you use your devices, but when you use them.**

Just like any addictive behavior, cutting back cold turkey doesn't usually work, so **it's best to gradually diminish the hours you are spending on your phone or tablet each day.** Use your phone's screen time feature to track how much time you spend per day on your phone and in what apps, then set targets to reduce the time spent in your top apps by 20 percent. Gradually increase that by 10 percent until you've cut your overall screen time in half. This could take weeks or months – it depends on the person and just how dedicated you are to being more responsible with your device (and just how addicted you were to begin with).

You can also help cut that time by being cognizant of when you are using your device. **Keeping your phone out of sight and out of use when you are in social settings or interacting with family at home has the added bonus of allowing you to reduce**

screen time and deepen your intimacy with loved ones. Instead of staring at a screen while you are with your partner or your friends, you can be fully engaged in the time you are spending with the people who are most important to you.

The same goes for situations where you are meeting new people – while the urge to lean on your phone as a social crutch may be intense, push past the awkwardness and find ways to connect. Ask questions, be sure to offer up affirmations that show you are actively engaged in someone's story, request more details to urge your conversation partner forward – in general, work on being a better conversationalist. It's a life skill that will suit you well in almost every aspect of your own life, from your relationship to your career.

Another time to be cognizant of your phone use is bedtime. **If you cut back anywhere on your screen time, make it the hours that lead to getting ready for sleep.** Knowing that cortisol is affected by your sleep cycle, and that the blue light of your screen disrupts your natural release of melatonin, it's only logical that limiting your exposure to screens before bedtime will help regulate your sleep cycle and, in turn, create a more restful sleep that will help balance out your cortisol.

Melatonin is directly tied to our circadian rhythm, meaning that when it starts getting dark out, our body signals that it's time to start winding down by releasing melatonin, which gradually makes us get sleepy. **If you are staring intently at a screen for hours after it gets dark, that is going to mess up that melatonin release and, in turn, your natural ability to fall asleep at the proper time when your cortisol is at its lowest.**

So, instead of scrolling through social media or answering emails after working hours, find other ways to wind down once the sun goes down. Read an actual physical book. Play a board game with your kids. Talk about your day with your spouse and make plans for the weekend. Pick up a new hobby and learn how to perfect it.

Whatever it is, the closer you get to bedtime, the less you should be looking at a screen – although ideally, there shouldn't be any phones or tablets in the picture once you've eaten dinner and settled down for the evening, but that can be a bridge too far for many. It's better to cut back and succeed than try to completely abstain, inevitably fail because you tried to do too much too soon, and then give up altogether and fall back into old patterns.

One of the easiest steps to take to kick off your new nighttime routine is to remove your phone from your bedroom. For many, this can result in an automatic hour or two of screen time immediately eliminated from your day – and at one of the most crucial junctures for ensuring your sleep isn't disturbed. Replace that nightly TikTok habit with a wind-down routine that focuses on promoting more restful, better quality sleep via journaling, meditation, or reflecting on your day.

Limiting your screen time isn't the only technology move to be mindful of – you'll also want to be conscious of what it is you are consuming when you are looking at your device.

If you are someone with anxiety or who is prone to catastrophizing, it's not in your best interest to seek out content that will exacerbate those anxieties and fears – especially at night. If you enjoy staring at the ceiling worrying endlessly about what could happen or imaginary doom scenarios until the late hours of the night, then by all means, go down that news alert rabbit hole at 10 p.m. But, as you can imagine, that's not going to do you or your mental health (or your sleep cycle) any favors.

If you can't seem to break your brain out of a "what if" loop, instead of indulging it with more fuel, try focusing on "what is" – be present in the now and on what is actually happening instead of your fears of what could happen. When faced with a stressful incident, when you keep thinking about what could have happened, your body will continue to exist in that stressed state, constantly preparing for more danger that could be around the bend – despite the fact that the danger has long since passed and is only in your mind as a possibility.

But, when you shift that thinking to instead think about what actually happened and move forward from the moment, it allows your body to recover and reset rather than continue to feel that stress over something that may never occur.

As cortisol gradually becomes a topic of interest for the general public, there will bound to be misinformation and misunderstandings around this Master Hormone.

The most important thing to realize is that you cannot completely eliminate stress from your life – cortisol spikes are out of your control because they are a basic physiological response to danger.

Cortisol is responsible for regulating so many of your body's functions and it's only natural to have a reaction to a stressful response. Stress as a whole is how our body keeps us safe from situations that are dangerous to our health.

What is not normal is existing in a perpetual state of chronic stress. Our bodies were not meant to be constantly in a fight or flight response with cortisol peaks happening late at night when it should be at its lowest point. The modern world – specifically with the dominance of technology – has fundamentally changed how our bodies function and caused a cortisol imbalance that requires a shift in how we interact with each other and our devices.

Technology is not going to move backwards. It's not going to slow down. While there are some minor guardrails being put in place, many of these changes happen far too late – well after the damage has been done. Meaning, if you want change, you need to orchestrate it yourself with thoughtful shifts in your own daily life.

There are proven, scientifically studied ways to balance and regulate cortisol – many of which I've discussed in this book – but far and away, **the habit that is going to have the most impact on managing stress and keeping your cortisol at its optimal cycle is to ensure that you are protecting your sleep.**

Going to bed when your cortisol is at its lowest point and rising as it hits its peak will help you get the deep, restful sleep you need to produce the hormones you need for the day ahead, so you can be prepared for whatever stressful situations arise in your inbox or between your kids when you roll out of bed in the morning.

You can't control stress – there will always be stressful situations in your life. But, you can control how prepared you are to react to those situations by ensuring that your body has all the tools it needs to both handle the stress and recover from it without long-lasting repercussions. You might not be able to be stress-free, but that doesn't mean you can't be stress-less.

To help you in reclaiming your life from technology and stress, here is the list of the tools I've recommended throughout this book:

Screens:

- Ideally no screens (TV, iPads, tablets, smart watches, computers, gaming) 1–2 hours before bed.

Food and fluids:

- Ideally not before 3–4 hours before bed (you want to empty your bowels before bed to prevent you from being woken up in your sleep to empty them. The older you get the more important this becomes).

- Eat healthy, farm to table, non-processed foods.

- Minimal sugar.
- Drink lots of fluids during the early morning and afternoon as so not need the bathroom during the night.
- No alcohol at night (cheat nights are to be expected). Your liver releases glucose into your bloodstream as needed to help keep your blood sugar at normal levels. When you drink alcohol, your liver needs to break down the alcohol. While your liver is processing alcohol, it stops releasing glucose.

Supplements:

- I would be doing you a disservice if I didn't remind you of the benefits of the various Rebalance Health lozenges in helping you manage your cortisol levels. The healthier your cortisol levels are, the easier it is to put your phone down and take back control of your life. To find the right Rebalance Health System for you, go to https://www.rebalancehealth.com.

Exercise:

- Ideally in the morning or afternoon.
- Evening workouts are not advised as exercise increases cortisol.
- No more than 90 minutes a day. Over-exercising is a red flag for increasing cortisol.

Sleep Hygiene:

- Go to bed approximately around the same time every day.
- Set yourself up for success by scheduling for 7–8 hours every night.
- Get into a routine to support winding down.

- Warm shower or bath.
- 64°–68° room temperature.
- White noise or 432Hz sleep music. (This music has been designed in 432Hz for relaxation, meditation, and healing purposes, to promote a sense of calmness, improve sleep quality, reduce stress, and anxiety).

About the Author

Justin Hai is a serial entrepreneur, product designer, and innovator whose career spans health, wellness, biotechnology, and skincare. He has co-founded multiple award-winning companies, including Alastin Skincare (acquired by Galderma in 2022), GLO Pharmaceuticals, and Rebalance Health.

Justin's deep dive into hormone health – especially the underappreciated role of cortisol – began with a desire to understand how modern stress impacts the body. That exploration ultimately led to the founding of Rebalance Health, a company focused on bringing science-backed solutions to help people regain control of their health. When his wife later faced a complex hormone-related condition that conventional medicine couldn't resolve, the mission became personal. Today, his work is driven by a commitment to help others find clarity, calm, and joy in their everyday lives.

With a degree in Industrial Design from the Rhode Island School of Design and an MBA from Pepperdine University, Justin blends creative vision with business strategy. He's contributed to projects for NASA, presented clean tech to the Pentagon, and holds multiple US patents and trademarks. His innovations have earned awards from International Design Awards, InStyle, Oprah, NewBeauty, Best in Biz, and NASA, among others.

Through his ventures and now through his writing, Justin continues to challenge the status quo – building products and stories that empower people to live and feel better from the inside out.

References

AACAP (2024). "Screen Time and Children," https://www.aacap.org/AACAP/Families_and_Youth/Facts_for_Families/FFF-Guide/Children-And-Watching-TV-054.aspx (accessed 24 April 2025).

Alkozei, A. et al. (2016). "Exposure to Blue Light Increases Subsequent Functional Activation of the Prefrontal Cortex During Performance of a Working Memory Task," *SLEEP* 39, no. 9: 1671–1680, 10.5665/sleep.6090.

Altuwairiqi, M., Jiang, N. and Ali, R. (2019). "Problematic Attachment to Social Media: Five Behavioural Archetypes," *International Journal of Environmental Research and Public Health* 16, no. 12: 2136, 10.3390/ijerph16122136.

America's Health Rankings (n.d.). "Explore Insufficient Sleep in the United States," https://www.americashealthrankings.org/explore/measures/sleep (accessed 23 April 2025).

American Academy of Pediatrics (2023). "Screen Time Guidelines," https://www.aap.org/en/patient-care/media-and-children/center-of-excellence-on-social-media-and-youth-mental-health/qa-portal/qa-portal-library/qa-portal-library-questions/screen-time-guidelines (accessed 24 April 2025).

American Psychiatric Association (2024). "American Adults Express Increasing Anxiousness in Annual Poll; Stress and Sleep Are Key Factors Impacting Mental Health," https://www.psychiatry.org/news-room/news-releases/annual-poll-adults-express-increasing-anxiousness (accessed 23 April 2025).

American Psychiatric Association (2025). "What Are Anxiety Disorders?," https://www.psychiatry.org/patients-families/anxiety-disorders/what-are-anxiety-disorders (accessed 24 April 2025).

American Psychological Association (2019). "Mindfulness Meditation," APA, October 30, 2019, https://www.apa.org/topics/mindfulness/meditation (accessed 25 April 2025).

Auld, F., Maschauer, E. L., Morrison, I., Skene, D. J. and Riha, R. L. (2016). "Evidence for the Efficacy of Melatonin in the Treatment of Primary Adult Sleep Disorders," *Sleep Medicine Reviews* 34: 10–22, 10.1016/j.smrv.2016.06.005.

Baumgartner, S. E., Weeda, W. D., van der Heijden, L. L. and Huizinga, M. (2014). "The Relationship Between Media Multitasking and Executive Function in Early Adolescents," *The Journal of Early Adolescence* 34, no. 8: 1120–1244, 10.1177/0272431614523133.

Beckers, T., Hermans, D., Lange, I., Luyten, L., Scheveneels, S. and Vervliet, B. (2023). "Understanding Clinical Fear and Anxiety Through the Lens of Human Fear Conditioning," *Nature Reviews Psychology* 2, no. 4: 233–245, 10.1038/s44159-023-00156-1.

Betteridge, B., Chien, W., Hazels, E. and Simone, J. (2023). "How Does Technology Affect the Attention Spans of Different Age Groups? | OxJournal," https://www.oxjournal.org/how-does-technology-affect-the-attention-spans-of-different-age-groups (accessed 24 April 2025).

Beukeboom, C. J. and Pollmann, M. (2021). "Partner Phubbing: Why Using Your Phone During Interactions with Your Partner Can Be Detrimental for Your Relationship." *Computers in Human Behavior*, 124: 106932, 10.1016/j.chb.2021.106932.

Bhattacharya, S. K., Goel, R. K., Kaur, R. and Ghosal, S. (1987). "Anti-stress Activity of Sitoindosides VII and VIII, New Acylsterylglucosides from *Withania somnifera*," *Phytotherapy Research* 1, no. 1: 32–37, 10.1002/ptr.2650010108.

Birdsall, T. C. (1998). "5-Hydroxytryptophan: A Clinically-effective Serotonin Precursor," *Alternative Medicine Review*, 3, no. 4: 271–280. Abstract at: https://pubmed.ncbi.nlm.nih.gov/9727088 (accessed 25 April 2025).

Blumberg, S. J., Luke, J. V. and National Center for Health Statistics (2024). "Wireless Substitution: Early Release of Estimates from the National Health Interview Survey, July-December 2023," *National Health Interview Survey Early Release Program*, https://www.cdc.gov/nchs/data/nhis/earlyrelease/wireless202406.pdf.

Boots (2021). "Vitamin Sales at Boots UK Surge as Customers Turn to Supplements to Support Their Wellbeing During Lockdown," https://www.boots-uk.com/newsroom/news/vitamin-sales-at-boots-uk-surge-as-customers-turn-to-supplements-to-support-their-wellbeing-during-lockdown (accessed 25 April 2025).

Bravo, R. et al. (2012). "Tryptophan-enriched Cereal Intake Improves Nocturnal Sleep, Melatonin, Serotonin, and Total Antioxidant Capacity Levels and Mood in Elderly Humans," *AGE* 35, no. 4: 1277–1285, 10.1007/s11357-012-9419-5.

Brenan, M. (2025). "Media Confidence in U.S. Matches 2016 Record Low," *Gallup.Com*, March 26, 2025, https://news.gallup.com/poll/512861/media-confidence-matches-2016-record-low.aspx (accessed 24 April 2025).

Buechler, J. (n.d.). "The Loneliness Epidemic Persists: A Post-Pandemic Look at the State of Loneliness Among U.S. Adults," The Cigna Group Newsroom, https://newsroom.thecignagroup.com/loneliness-epidemic-persists-post-pandemic-look (accessed 24 April 2025).

Bühler, J. L., Krauss, S. and Orth, U. (2021). "Development of Relationship Satisfaction Across the Life Span: A Systematic Review and Meta-Analysis," *Psychological Bulletin,* 147, no. 10: 1012–1053, 10.1037/bul0000342.

Calabrese, C., Gregory, W. L., Leo, M., Kraemer, D., Bone, K. and Oken, B. (2008). "Effects of a Standardized Bacopa Monnieri Extract on Cognitive Performance, Anxiety, and Depression in the Elderly: A Randomized, Double-Blind, Placebo-Controlled Trial," *The Journal of Alternative and Complementary Medicine* 14, no. 6: 707–713, 10.1089/acm.2008.0018.

CDC (2022). "QuickStats: Percentage of Adults Aged ≥18 Years Who Sleep <7 Hours on Average in a 24-Hour Period, by Sex and Age Group – National Health Interview Survey, United States, 2020," *MMWR Morbidity and Mortality Weekly Report* 71, no. 10: 393, 10.15585/mmwr.mm7110a6.

Chai, S. C., Li, I., Pacanowski, C. and Brewer, B. (2020). "Effects of Four-Week Supplementation of Ashwagandha and B-Vitamins on Mood and Stress Relief," *Current Developments in Nutrition* 4: nzaa057_011, 10.1093/cdn/nzaa057_011.

Chan, I. I. and Wu, A. M. S. (2024). "Assessing the Role of Cortisol in Anxiety, Major Depression, and Neuroticism: A Mendelian Randomization Study Using *SERPINA6/SERPINA1* Variants," *Biological Psychiatry: Global Open Science*, 4, no. 3: 100294, https://www.bpsgos.org/article/S2667-1743(24)00007-7/fulltext (accessed 24 April 2025).

Chan, S. and Debono, M. (2010). "Review: Replication of Cortisol Circadian Rhythm: New Advances in Hydrocortisone Replacement Therapy," *Therapeutic Advances in Endocrinology and Metabolism* 1, no. 3: 129–38, 10.1177/2042018810380214.

Chen, C.-R., Zhou, X.-Z., Luo, Y.-J., Huang, Z.-L., Urade, Y. and Wei-Min, Q. (2012). "Magnolol, a Major Bioactive Constituent of the Bark of *Magnolia officinalis*, Induces Sleep Via the Benzodiazepine Site of $GABA_A$ Receptor in Mice," *Neuropharmacology*, 63, no. 6: 1191–1199. 10.1016/j.neuropharm.2012.06.031.

Choudhary, D., Bhattacharyya, S. and Bose, S. (2017). "Efficacy and Safety of Ashwagandha (*Withania somnifera* (L.) Dunal) Root Extract in Improving Memory and Cognitive Functions," *Journal of Dietary Supplements* 14, no. 6: 599–612, 10.1080/19390211.2017.1284970.

Cleveland Clinic (2025a). "Anxiety Disorders," https://my.clevelandclinic.org/health/diseases/9536-anxiety-disorders (accessed 24 April 2025).

Cleveland Clinic (2025b). "Cortisol," Cleveland Clinic, February 17, 2025, https://my.clevelandclinic.org/health/articles/22187-cortisol (accessed 23 April 2025).

Cox, D. A. (2021). "The State of American Friendship: Change, Challenges, and Loss," The Survey Center on American Life, March 10, 2025, https://www.americansurveycenter.org/research/the-state-of-american-friendship-change-challenges-and-loss (accessed 24 April 2025).

C-SPAN (2023). "OpenAI CEO Testifies on Artificial Intelligence," *C-SPAN. Org*, https://www.c-span.org/program/senate-committee/openai-ceo-testifies-on-artificial-intelligence/627836 (accessed 25 April 2025).

CTA (2024). "CTA Research: Exploring Gen Z Views and Preferences in Technology," https://www.cta.tech/press-releases/cta-research-exploring-gen-z-views-and-preferences-in-technology (accessed 24 April 2025).

Dakanalis, A. et al. (2023). "The Association of Emotional Eating with Overweight/Obesity, Depression, Anxiety/Stress, and Dietary Patterns: A Review of the Current Clinical Evidence," *Nutrients* 15, no. 5: 1173, 10.3390/nu15051173.

Dasdelen, M. F. et al. (2022). "A Novel Theanine Complex, Mg-L-Theanine Improves Sleep Quality via Regulating Brain Electrochemical Activity," *Frontiers in Nutrition* 9, 10.3389/fnut.2022.874254.

DePolo, J. (2025). "Menopause and Menopausal Symptoms," January 22, 2025, https://www.breastcancer.org/treatment-side-effects/menopause (accessed 24 April 2025).

Deshpande, A., Irani, N., Balkrishnan, R. and Benny, I. R. (2020). "A Randomized, Double Blind, Placebo Controlled Study to Evaluate the Effects of Ashwagandha (*Withania somnifera*) Extract on Sleep Quality in Healthy Adults," *Sleep Medicine* 72 (March 21, 2020): 28–36, 10.1016/j.sleep.2020.03.012.

DiJulio, B., Hamel, L., Muñana, C. and Brodie, M. (2018). "Loneliness and Social Isolation in the United States, the United Kingdom, and Japan: An International Survey," KFF, August 30, 2018, https://www.kff.org/mental-health/report/loneliness-and-social-isolation-in-the-united-states-the-united-kingdom-and-japan-an-international-survey (accessed 24 April 2025).

Ditzen, B. et al. (2007). "Effects of Different Kinds of Couple Interaction on Cortisol and Heart Rate Responses to Stress in Women," *Psychoneuroendocrinology* 32, no. 5: 565–574, 10.1016/j.psyneuen.2007.03.011.

Dording, C. M. et al. (2015). "A Double-Blind Placebo-Controlled Trial of Maca Root as Treatment for Antidepressant-Induced Sexual Dysfunction in Women," *Evidence-Based Complementary and Alternative Medicine* 2015: 1–9, 10.1155/2015/949036.

Dreisoerner, A. et al. (2021). "Self-soothing Touch and Being Hugged Reduce Cortisol Responses to Stress: A Randomized Controlled Trial on Stress, Physical Touch, and Social Identity," *Comprehensive Psychoneuroendocrinology* 8: 100091, 10.1016/j.cpnec.2021.100091.

Dwyer, R. J., Kushlev, K. and Dunn, E. W. (2018) "Smartphone Use Undermines Enjoyment of Face to Face Social Interactions," *Journal of Experimental Social Psychology*, 78: 233–239. 10.1016/j.jesp.2017.10.007.

Eastman, C. and Smith, N. (2012). "Shift Work: Health, Performance and Safety Problems, Traditional Countermeasures, and Innovative Management Strategies to Reduce Circadian Misalignment," *Nature and Science of Sleep*, 111, 10.2147/nss.s10372.

Eby, G. A. Davis, D. R. and Halcomb, W. W. (1984). "Reduction in Duration of Common Colds by Zinc Gluconate Lozenges in a Double-blind Study," *Antimicrobial Agents and Chemotherapy* 25, no. 1: 20–24, 10.1128/aac.25.1.20.

Figueiro, M. G. and Rea, M. S. (2010). "The Effects of Red and Blue Lights on Circadian Variations in Cortisol, Alpha Amylase, and Melatonin," *International Journal of Endocrinology*, 2010, 1–9, 10.1155/2010/829351.

Fioroni, S. and Foy, D. (2025). "Americans Sleeping Less, More Stressed," *Gallup.Com*, March 26, 2025, https://news.gallup.com/poll/642704/americans-sleeping-less-stressed.aspx (accessed 23 April 2025).

Fish, R. (2024). "The Internet Is Trauma-Dumping on Elmo," *The Hollywood Reporter*, February 2, 2024, https://www.hollywoodreporter.com/news/general-news/elmo-how-are-you-doing-twitter-1235811025 (accessed 24 April 2025).

Freedman, G., Powell, D. N., Le, B. and Williams, K. D. (2018). "Ghosting and Destiny: Implicit Theories of Relationships Predict Beliefs About Ghosting," *Journal of Social and Personal Relationships* 36, no. 3: 905–924, 10.1177/0265407517748791.

Gelles-Watnick, R. (2024). "Americans' Use of Mobile Technology and Home Broadband," Pew Research Center, July 22, 2024, https://www.pewresearch.org/internet/2024/01/31/americans-use-of-mobile-technology-and-home-broadband (accessed 25 April 2025).

Golen, T. and Ricciotti, H. (2022). "Could Stress Be Making My Acid Reflux Worse?," Harvard Health, May 1, 2022, https://www.health.harvard.edu/diseases-and-conditions/could-stress-be-making-my-acid-reflux-worse (accessed 23 April 2025).

Gonzales, G. F. et al. (2002). "Effect of *Lepidium meyenii* (MACA) on Sexual Desire and Its Absent Relationship with Serum Testosterone Levels in Adult Healthy Men," *Andrologia* 34, no. 6: 367–372, 10.1046/j.1439-0272.2002.00519.x.

Guo, S.-S. et al. (2016). "Preservation of Cognitive Function by Lepidium Meyenii (Maca) Is Associated with Improvement of Mitochondrial Activity and Upregulation of Autophagy-Related Proteins in Middle-Aged Mouse Cortex," *Evidence-Based Complementary and Alternative Medicine* 2016, no. 1, 10.1155/2016/4394261.

Gupta, M. and Sharma, A. (2021). "Fear of Missing Out: A Brief Overview of Origin, Theoretical Underpinnings and Relationship with Mental Health," *World Journal of Clinical Cases* 9, no. 19: 4881–4889, 10.12998/wjcc.v9.i19.4881.

Haddock, A., Ward, N., Yu, R. and O'Dea, N. (2022). "Positive Effects of Digital Technology Use by Adolescents: A Scoping Review of the Literature," *International Journal of Environmental Research and Public Health* 19, no. 21: 14009, 10.3390/ijerph192114009.

Hajak, G. et al. (1991). "The Influence of Intravenous L-Tryptophan on Plasma Melatonin and Sleep in Men," *Pharmacopsychiatry* 24, no. 1: 17–20, 10.1055/s-2007-1014427.

Haupt, S., Eckstein, M. L., Wolf, A., Zimmer, R. T., Wachsmuth, N. B. and Moser, O. (2021). "Eat, Train, Sleep—Retreat? Hormonal Interactions of Intermittent Fasting, Exercise and Circadian Rhythm," *Biomolecules* 11, no. 4: 516, 10.3390/biom11040516.

Hobbs, M., Owen, S. and Gerber, L. (2016). "Liquid Love? Dating Apps, Sex, Relationships and the Digital Transformation of Intimacy," *Journal of Sociology* 53, no. 2: 271–284, 10.1177/1440783316662718.

Holt-Lunstad, J. (2017). "Why Social Relationships Are Important for Physical Health: A Systems Approach to Understanding and Modifying Risk and Protection," *Annual Review of Psychology* 69, no. 1: 437–458, 10.1146/annurev-psych-122216-011902.

IARC (2020). "*IARC Monographs* Volume 124: Night Shift Work," https://www.iarc.who.int/news-events/iarc-monographs-volume-124-night-shift-work (accessed 23 April 2025).

Iyengar, S. S. and Lepper, M. R. (2000). "When Choice Is Demotivating: Can One Desire Too Much of a Good Thing?," *Journal of Personality and Social Psychology* 79, no. 6: 995–1006, 10.1037/0022-3514.79.6.995.

Johns Hopkins Medicine (2025). "Can Menopause Cause Depression?," https://www.hopkinsmedicine.org/health/wellness-and-prevention/can-menopause-cause-depression (accessed 24 April 2025).

Jung, C. M. et al. (2010). "Acute Effects of Bright Light Exposure on Cortisol Levels," *Journal of Biological Rhythms* 25, no. 3: 208–16, 10.1177/0748730410368413.

Kalman, D. S., Feldman, S., Feldman, R., Schwartz, H. I., Krieger, D. R. and Garrison, R. (2008). "Effect of a Proprietary Magnolia and Phellodendron extract on Stress Levels in Healthy Women: A Pilot, Double-blind, Placebo-controlled Clinical Trial," *Nutrition Journal* 7, no. 1, 10.1186/1475-2891-7-11.

Kardeş, E. and Kardeş, S. (2021). "Google Searches for Bruxism, Teeth Grinding, and Teeth Clenching During the COVID-19 Pandemic," *Journal of Orofacial Orthopedics/Fortschritte Der Kieferorthopädie* 83, no. 6: 1–6, 10.1007/s00056-021-00315-0.

Kassel, G. (2024). "How Does Exercise Affect Cortisol Levels?," *Shape*, May 12, 2024, https://www.shape.com/fitness/tips/high-cortisol-levels-exercise-stress (accessed 25 April 2025).

Kemp, S. (2025). "Digital 2024: Global Overview Report," DataReportal – Global Digital Insights, March 23, 2025, https://datareportal.com/reports/digital-2024-global-overview-report (accessed 24 April 2025).

Kennedy, D. O. et al. (2020). "Acute and Chronic Effects of Green Oat (Avena Sativa) Extract on Cognitive Function and Mood During a Laboratory Stressor in Healthy Adults: A Randomised, Double-Blind, Placebo-Controlled Study in Healthy Humans," *Nutrients* 12, no. 6: 1598, 10.3390/nu12061598.

Kim, S.-K., Kim, S.-Y. and Kang, H.-B. (2016). "An Analysis of the Effects of Smartphone Push Notifications on Task Performance with Regard to Smartphone Overuse Using ERP," *Computational Intelligence and Neuroscience* 2016: 1–8, 10.1155/2016/5718580.

Kling, J. M. et al. (2019). "Menopause Management Knowledge in Postgraduate Family Medicine, Internal Medicine, and Obstetrics and Gynecology Residents: A Cross-Sectional Survey." *Mayo Clinic Proceedings*, 94, no. 2: 242–253. https://www.mayoclinicproceedings.org/article/S0025-6196(18)30701-8/abstract (accessed 24 April 2025).

Klucharev, V., Hytönen, K., Rijpkema, M., Smidts, A. and Fernández, G. (2009). "Reinforcement Learning Signal Predicts Social Conformity," *Neuron* 61, no. 1: 140–151, 10.1016/j.neuron.2008.11.027.

Kroencke, L., Harari, G. M., Back, M. D. and Wagner, J. (2023). "Well-being in Social Interactions: Examining Personality-situation Dynamics in Face-to-face and Computer-mediated Communication," *Journal of Personality and Social Psychology* 124, no. 2: 437–460, 10.1037/pspp0000422.

Kushlev, K., Hunter, J. F., Proulx, J., Pressman, S. D. and Dunn, E. (2019). "Smartphones Reduce Smiles Between Strangers," *Computers in Human Behavior* 91: 12–16, 10.1016/j.chb.2018.09.023.

Liao, L.-Y. et al. (2018). "A Preliminary Review of Studies on Adaptogens: Comparison of Their Bioactivity in TCM with That of Ginseng-like Herbs Used Worldwide," *Chinese Medicine* 13, no. 1, 10.1186/s13020-018-0214-9.

Lin, B. and Li, S. (2011). "*Cordyceps* as an Herbal Drug." *Herbal Medicine: Biomolecular and Clinical Aspects*, 2nd edition: chapter 5. https://www.ncbi.nlm.nih.gov/books/NBK92758/?ref=ollie (accessed 25 April 2025).

Lockley, S. W., Brainard, G. C. and Czeisler, C. A. (2003). "High Sensitivity of the Human Circadian Melatonin Rhythm to Resetting by Short Wavelength Light," *The Journal of Clinical Endocrinology & Metabolism*, 88, no. 9: 4502–4505. 10.1210/jc.2003-030570.

Manfredini, D., Winocur, E., Guarda-Nardini, L., Paesani, D. and Lobbezoo, F. (2013). "Epidemiology of Bruxism in Adults: A Systematic Review of the Literature," *Journal of Orofacial Pain* 27, no. 2: 99–110, 10.11607/jop.921.

Mastroianni, A. C., Faden, R. and Federman, D. (1994). "NIH Revitalization Act of 1993 Public Law 103-43," Women and Health Research - NCBI Bookshelf, https://www.ncbi.nlm.nih.gov/books/NBK236531 (accessed 24 April 2025).

McClure, S. M., Berns, G. S. and Read Montague, P. (2003). "Temporal Prediction Errors in a Passive Learning Task Activate Human Striatum," *Neuron* 38, no. 2: 339–346, 10.1016/s0896-6273(03)00154-5.

McCraty, R., Barrios-Choplin, B., Rozman, D., Atkinson, M. and Watkins, A. D. (1998). "The Impact of a New Emotional Self-management Program on Stress, Emotions, Heart Rate Variability, DHEA and Cortisol," *Integrative Physiological and Behavioral Science* 33, no. 2: 151–70, 10.1007/bf02688660.

Misra, S., Cheng, L., Genevie, J. and Yuan, M. (2014). "The iPhone Effect," *Environment and Behavior* 48, no. 2: 275–98, 10.1177/0013916514539755.

Monninger, M. et al. (2023) "The Importance of High Quality Real-life Social Interactions During the COVID-19 Pandemic," *Scientific Reports* 13, no. 1, 10.1038/s41598-023-30803-9.

Muppalla, S. K., Vuppalapati, S., Pulliahgaru, A. R. and Sreenivasulu (2023). "Effects of Excessive Screen Time on Child Development: An Updated Review and Strategies for Management," *Cureus*, 10.7759/cureus.40608.

Murthy, V. H. (2023). "Our Epidemic of Loneliness and Isolation: The U.S. Surgeon General's Advisory on the Healing Effects of Social Connection and Community," https://www.hhs.gov/sites/default/files/surgeon-general-social-connection-advisory.pdf (accessed 24 April 2025).

Nagata, A., Tajima, T. and Uchida, M. (2006). "Supplemental Anti-fatigue Effects of *Cordyceps sinensis* (Tochu-Kaso) Extract Powder During Three Stepwise Exercise of Human." *Japanese Journal of Physical Fitness and Sports Medicine* 55 Supplement: S145–S152, https://www.jstage.jst.go.jp/article/jspfsm/55/Supplement/55_S145/_pdf/-char/en? (accessed 25 April 2025).

Nassar, E. et al. (2007). "Effects of a Single Dose of N-Acetyl-5-methoxytryptamine (Melatonin) and Resistance Exercise on the Growth Hormone/IGF-1 Axis in Young Males and Females," *Journal of the International Society of Sports Nutrition* 4, no. 1, 10.1186/1550-2783-4-14.

National Alliance on Mental Illness (2025). "Anxiety Disorders | NAMI," NAMI, January 3, 2025, https://www.nami.org/About-Mental-Illness/Mental-Health-Conditions/Anxiety-Disorders (accessed 24 April 2025).

National Cancer Institute (2022). "Electromagnetic Fields and Cancer," Cancer.gov, May 30, 2022, https://www.cancer.gov/about-cancer/causes-prevention/risk/radiation/electromagnetic-fields-fact-sheet (accessed 25 April 2025).

National Center for Health Statistics (n.d.). "FastStats," Marriage and Divorce, https://www.cdc.gov/nchs/fastats/marriage-divorce.htm (accessed 24 April 2025).

National Sleep Foundation (2024). "How Much Sleep Do You Really Need?," National Sleep Foundation, August 30, 2024, https://www.thensf.org/how-many-hours-of-sleep-do-you-really-need (accessed 23 April 2025).

Navarro, R., Larrañaga, E., Yubero, S. and Villora, B. (2020). "Psychological Correlates of Ghosting and Breadcrumbing Experiences: A Preliminary Study Among Adults," *International Journal of Environmental Research and Public Health* 17, no. 3: 1116, 10.3390/ijerph17031116.

Nie, N. H. and Erbring, L. (2002). "Internet and Society: A Preliminary Report," *IT&Society*, 1, no. 1: 275–283, http://143.107.236.240/documentos/textos/cultura_digital/tics_arq_urb/internet_society%20report.pdf (accessed 24 April 2025).

O'Connor, A. (2015). "New York Attorney General Targets Supplements at Major Retailers," Well, February 3, 2015, https://archive.nytimes.com/well.blogs.nytimes.com/2015/02/03/new-york-attorney-general-targets-supplements-at-major-retailers (accessed 25 April 2025).

O'Doherty, J. P. (2004). "Reward Representations and Reward-related Learning in the Human Brain: Insights from Neuroimaging," *Current Opinion in Neurobiology* 14, no. 6: 769–776, 10.1016/j.conb.2004.10.016.

Office of Dietary Supplements (1994). "Dietary Supplement Health and Education Act of 1994," https://ods.od.nih.gov/About/DSHEA_Wording.aspx (accessed 25 April 2025).

Oliveri, F. et al. (2020). "Role of Depression and Anxiety Disorders in Takotsubo Syndrome: The Psychiatric Side of Broken Heart," *Cureus*, 10.7759/cureus.10400.

O'Neill, M. T., Jones, V. and Reid, A. (2023). "Impact of Menopausal Symptoms on Work and Careers: A Cross-sectional Study," *Occupational Medicine* 73, no. 6: 332–338, 10.1093/occmed/kqad078.

Ozbay, F., Johnson, D. C., Dimoulas, E., Morgan III, C. A., Charney, D. and Southwick, S. (2007). "Social Support and Resilience to Stress: From Neurobiology to Clinical Practice," *Psychiatry*, 4, no. 5: 35–40, https://pmc.ncbi.nlm.nih.gov/articles/PMC2921311 (accessed 24 April 2025).

Packheiser, J., Hartmann, H., Fredriksen, K., Gazzola, V., Keysers, C. and Michon, F. (2024). "A Systematic Review and Multivariate Meta-analysis of the Physical and Mental Health Benefits of Touch Interventions," *Nature Human Behaviour* 8, no. 6: 1088–1107, 10.1038/s41562-024-01841-8.

Peiró-Velert, C., Valencia-Peris, A., González, L. M., Garcia-Massó, X., Serra-Añó, P. and Devis-Devis, J. (2014). "Screen Media Usage, Sleep Time and Academic Performance in Adolescents: Clustering a Self-Organizing Maps Analysis," *PLoS ONE* 9, no. 6: e99478, 10.1371/journal.pone.0099478.

Peth-Nui, T. et al. (2012). "Effects of 12-Week *Bacopa monnieri* Consumption on Attention, Cognitive Processing, Working Memory, and Functions of Both Cholinergic and Monoaminergic Systems in Healthy Elderly Volunteers," *Evidence-Based Complementary and Alternative Medicine* 2012: 1–10, 10.1155/2012/606424.

Pitt, S. (2024). "Just the Numbers: The Surge of Supplement Sales," *BeautyMatter*, July 19, 2024, https://beautymatter.com/articles/the-surge-of-supplement-sales (accessed 25 April 2025).

Polaris Market Research (2025). "Sleeping Aids Market Analysis: Size & Global Trends Report 2034," https://www.polarismarketresearch.com/industry-analysis/sleeping-aids-market (accessed 23 April 2025).

Psychology Today (2018). "JOMO: The Joy of Missing Out," https://www.psychologytoday.com/us/blog/happiness-is-state-mind/201807/jomo-the-joy-missing-out.

Rao, T. P., Ozeki, M. and Juneja, L. R. (2015). "In Search of a Safe Natural Sleep Aid," *Journal of the American College of Nutrition* 34, no. 5: 436–447, 10.1080/07315724.2014.926153.

Rebalance Health, Inc. (2024). "North American Menopause Society Publishes Rebalance Health IRB Study Citing an 80% Efficacy in the Reduction of Hot Flashes," October 16, 2024, https://rebalancehealth.com/blogs/press-releases/north-american-menopause-society-publishes-rebalancehealth-irb-study-citing-an-80-efficacy-in-the-reduction-of-hot-flashes? (accessed 25 April 2025).

Rebalance Health, Inc. (2025). "Journal of Nutraceuticals and Food Science," February 19, 2025, https://rebalancehealth.com/blogs/publications/journal-of-nutraceuticals-and-food-science?srsltid=AfmBOoqKwX1rgNH_rbILa49TpV6TyuUyPtiRn6mO7MzLNbBfRcfxAfWs (accessed 25 April 2025).

Sarris, J. et al., (2018). "L-theanine in the Adjunctive Treatment of Generalized Anxiety Disorder: A Double-blind, Randomised, Placebo-controlled Trial," *Journal of Psychiatric Research* 110: 31–37, 10.1016/j.jpsychires.2018.12.014.

Sbarra, D. A., Briskin, J. L. and Slatcher, R. B. (2019). "Smartphones and Close Relationships: The Case for an Evolutionary Mismatch," *Perspectives on Psychological Science* 14, no. 4: 596–618, 10.1177/1745691619826535.

Schaefer, V. E. (1998). *The Care & Keeping of You: The Body Book for Girls*. Middleton, WI: American Girl Publishing.

Schneider, E. et al. (2023). "Affectionate Touch and Diurnal Oxytocin Levels: An Ecological Momentary Assessment Study," *eLife* 12, 10.7554/elife.81241.

ScienceDaily (2007). "Unsupervised Children Are More Sociable and More Active, Study Says," ScienceDaily, December 7, 2007, https://www.sciencedaily.com/releases/2007/12/071218192030.htm (accessed 24 April 2025).

Sesame Workshop (2024). "Sesame Workshop and the Harris Poll Unveil Inaugural Index on the State of America's Well-Being," August 13, 2024, https://sesameworkshop.org/about-us/press-room/sesame-workshop-and-the-harris-poll-unveil-inaugural-index-on-the-state-of-americas-well-being (accessed 24 April 2025).

Simpson, T., Pase, M. and Stough, C. (2015). "*Bacopa monnieri* as an Antioxidant Therapy to Reduce Oxidative Stress in the Aging Brain," *Evidence-Based Complementary and Alternative Medicine* 2015: 1–9, 10.1155/2015/615384.

Singer, N. (2024). "Teen Girls Confront an Epidemic of Deepfake Nudes in Schools," *The New York Times*, April 8, 2024, https://www.nytimes

.com/2024/04/08/technology/deepfake-ai-nudes-westfield-high-school .html (accessed 24 April 2024).

Smiderle, F. R. et al. (2014). "Anti-Inflammatory Properties of the Medicinal Mushroom *Cordyceps militaris* Might Be Related to Its Linear (1→3)-β-D-Glucan," *PLoS ONE* 9, no. 10: e110266, 10.1371/journal. pone.0110266.

Society for Women's Health Research (2025). "Menopause," January 30, 2025, https://swhr.org/health_focus_area/menopause (accessed 24 April 2025).

Stothart, C., Mitchum, A. and Yehnert, C. (2015). "The Attentional Cost of Receiving a Cell Phone Notification," *Journal of Experimental Psychology: Human Perception and Performance,* 41, no. 4: 893–897, 10.1037/ xhp0000100.

Stratatkis, C. A. (2006). "Cortisol and Growth Hormone: Clinical Implications of a Complex, Dynamic Relationship," *Pediatric Endocrinology Reviews* 3, 333–338.

Tang, W. et al. (2005). "A Randomized, Double-Blind and Placebo-Controlled Study of a Ganoderma lucidum Polysaccharide Extract in Neurasthenia," *Journal of Medicinal Food* 8, no. 1: 53–58, 10.1089/jmf.2005.8.53.

The Conversation (2015). "Is HRT Safe to Use for the Menopause? What the Science Says," https://www.ox.ac.uk/research/hrt-safe-use-menopause-what-science-says-0 (accessed 24 April 2025).

The Cut (2023). "194 Modern Etiquette Rules for Life After COVID," https:// www.thecut.com/article/tipping-rules-etiquette-rules.html (accessed 25 April 2025).

Thomson, C. A., Ho, E. and Strom, M. B. (2016). "Chemopreventive Properties of 3,3'-diindolylmethane in Breast Cancer: Evidence from Experimental and Human Studies," *Nutrition Reviews* 74, no. 7: 432–443, 10.1093/nutrit/nuw010.

Tomova, L., Tye, K. and Saxe, R. (2019). "The Neuroscience of Unmet Social Needs," *Social Neuroscience* 16, no. 3: 221–31, 10.1080/ 17470919.2019.1694580.

Triscoli, C., Cray, I., Olausson, H. and Sailer, U. (2017). "Touch Between Romantic Partners: Being Stroked Is More Pleasant Than Stroking and

Decelerates Heart Rate," *Physiology & Behavior* 177: 169–175, 10.1016/j.physbeh.2017.05.006.

UCLA Health (2022). "Should You Take Gummy Vitamins?," UCLA Health, December 12, 2022, https://www.uclahealth.org/news/article/should-you-take-gummy-vitamins (accessed 25 April 2025).

Uncapher, M. R. et al. (2017). "Media Multitasking and Cognitive, Psychological, Neural, and Learning Differences," *PEDIATRICS* 140, no. 2: S62–S66, 10.1542/peds.2016-1758d.

US Surgeon General (2023). "Social Media and Youth Mental Health: The U.S. Surgeon General's Advisory," https://www.hhs.gov/sites/default/files/sg-youth-mental-health-social-media-advisory.pdf (accessed 24 April 2025).

Vanden Abeele, M. M. P., Antheunis, M. L. and Schouten, A. P. (2016). "The Effect of Mobile Messaging During a Conversation on Impression Formation and Interaction Quality," *Computers in Human Behavior*, 62: 562–569. 10.1016/j.chb.2016.04.005.

Vision Direct (n.d.). "How Much Time Do We Spend Looking at Screens?," https://www.visiondirect.co.uk/blog/research-reveals-screen-time-habits (accessed 23 April 2025).

Weiss, H. (2022). "Why You're Grinding Your Teeth—And How to Stop," *TIME*, September 8, 2022, https://time.com/6211613/how-to-stop-grinding-teeth-bruxism (accessed 24 April 2025).

Wieczorek, L. L., Chivers, M., Koehn, M. A., DeBruine, L. M. and Jones, B. C. (2022). "Age Effects on Women's and Men's Dyadic and Solitary Sexual Desire," *Archives of Sexual Behavior* 51, no. 8 (August 2, 2022): 3765–3789, 10.1007/s10508-022-02375-8.

Wiedenmayer, C. P., Bansal, R., Anderson, G. M., Zhu, H., Amat, J., Whiteman, R. and Peterson, B. S. (2006). "Cortisol Levels and Hippocampus Volumes in Healthy Preadolescent Children," *Biological Psychiatry* 60, no. 8: 856–861, 10.1016/j.biopsych.2006.02.011.

Woodbury, A., Yu, S.-P., Wei, L. and Garcia, P. (2013). "Neuro-Modulating Effects of Honokiol: A Review," *Frontiers in Neurology* 4, 10.3389/fneur.2013.00130.

Wolff, J. (2018). "What Doctors Don't Know About Menopause," AARP, July 20, 2018, https://www.aarp.org/health/conditions-treatments/menopause-symptoms-doctors-relief-treatment (accessed 24 April 2025).

Wood, A. M., Joseph, S., Lloyd, J. and Atkins, S. (2008). "Gratitude Influences Sleep Through the Mechanism of Pre-sleep Cognitions," *Journal of Psychosomatic Research* 66, no. 1: 43–48, 10.1016/j.jpsychores.2008.09.002.

World Health Organization (2018). "Public Health Implications of Excessive Use of the Internet and Other Communication and Gaming Platforms," Press release, September 13, 2018, https://www.who.int/news/item/13-09-2018-public-health-implications-of-excessive-use-of-the-internet-and-other-communication-and-gaming-platforms (accessed 24 April 2025).

Yale School of Medicine (2022). "Sleep's Crucial Role in Preserving Memory," https://medicine.yale.edu/news-article/sleeps-crucial-role-in-preserving-memory (accessed 23 April 2025).

Yoon, S. and Lee, K.-P. (2015). "A Study on Notification System Design of Smartphone Messenger Considering the User's Stress," *Archives of Design Research* 28, no. 2: 75, 10.15187/adr.2015.05.28.2.75.

Zisapel, N. (2018). "New Perspectives on the Role of Melatonin in Human Sleep, Circadian Rhythms and Their Regulation," *British Journal of Pharmacology* 175, no. 16: 3190–3199, 10.1111/bph.14116.

Index

5-Hydroxytryptophan (5-HTP), L-Tryptophan conversion, 183–184

A
Adaptogens/herbs/botanicals, providing, 21–22
Addison's disease, 18–19
Adrenaline, trigger, 8–9
Algorithms, negative impact, 83–85, 105–106
Andropause, 55
Angry silence, problem, 212
Anxiety
    abnormality, 78–79
    avoidance, JOMO (impact), 196
    chronic stress, contrast, 85–86
    cortisol, impact, 75
    development, 81
    disorders, 76
    exposure, 82–83
    external trigger, absence, 77
    media depiction, 75–76
    relief, technology (usage), 82–83
    stress, contrast, 76–78
    understanding, 79–82
Apple, Focus/Do Not Disturb (addition), 104
Apprehensiveness, FOMO (impact), 193
Artificial intelligence (AI), impact, 108–109
Ashwagandha (Superceutical ingredient), 181–182
Attachment, problems, 193
Attention, preciousness, 137
Avena sativa stems/leaves, usage, 185–186
Avoidance behaviors, 82

B
Bacopa (Superceutical ingredient), 182
Bedroom
    no-device zone, 203–205
    phone, removal, 204–205, 216
    sleep/sex focus, 44

Bedtime
  cortisol levels, attention, 218
  practices, 124–127
Biological Psychiatry: Global Open Science (study), 81
Blue light, impact, 40, 95, 98–101
Body
  natural rhythms (support), Rebalance lozenges (usage), 189–190
  optimal function, 17
  physiological response, creation, 87
  sleep schedule, regularity (requirement), 30–32
  smartphones, impact, 98
  stress response, 80
Bone health, menopause (impact), 65
Botox, usage, 69–70
Brain
  fog (avoidance), JOMO (usage), 191
  glands, presence, 6
  multitasking, negative impact, 120–121
  what if loop, escape, 216–217
Broken sleep (avoidance), JOMO (usage), 191
Bruxism, stress/anxiety (link), 15
Burnout (avoidance), JOMO (usage), 191

C
Children
  artificial intelligence (AI), usage, 130
  bedtime, practices, 124–127
  development, 212
  media images, misunderstanding, 117
  media usage, moderation, 127–128
  motivation (death), multitasking (impact), 120–121
  online time, adult online time (contrast), 118–119
  parents
    example, setting, 128–129
    involvement, 126–127
  roaming/unsupervised play, loss, 114
  screens (impact)
    knowledge, insufficiency, 114–115
    school battles, 122–123
  screen time, excess (negative impact), 110–111
  self-worth, determination, 116
  sleep, priority, 123–124
  smartphones, negative impact, 113
  social media
    danger, 116–117
    impact, 115–116

240
Index

targeting, adult predators
(impact), 117–118
Chronic stress
anxiety, contrast, 85–86
impact, 75
perpetual existence,
abnormality, 217–218
understanding, 79–82
Circadian sleep, setting, 30
Clickbait, negative impact, 83–85
Clinically tested ingredients,
absence/limitations,
178–179
Cognitive behavioral therapy
(CBT), 82, 208
Collie, Wendy, 132–135
Conversation
distraction, smartphones
(impact), 164–165
partnership, importance, 149
Cookies (Internet), impact,
105–106
Cordyceps mushrooms
(Superceutical
ingredient), 182
Cortisol
aging/menopause,
relationship, 19–21
balance
face-to-face interactions,
positive impact, 136–137
solution, 22–23

depression, association, 81
endings, loss, 12–14
high levels, 8–11
impact, 7–8
increase, 64, 168, 169
blue light, impact, 40
smartphones, impact, 43–44
stress/chronic stress/
anxiety, impact, 75
levels, control, 218
management
Rebalance Health products,
usage, 72–73
technology, usage, 214–220
master hormone, 3
reason, 5–8
natural rhythm, disruption, 3
overload, normalcy, 14
peaks, 29
problems, 10
production, 7, 54
push notifications, impact,
101–103
receptor, presence, 5
reduction, 208
physical touch, impact,
159–161
regulation, 45, 125
rhythms (optimization),
Rebalance
Superceuticals® Lozenges
(usage), 175

Cortisol (*continued*)
   stress/insulin resistance, relationship, 15–16
   technology/sleep, correlation, 13
   trigger, 8–11
Couples
   relationship, cell phone interference, 168
Couples, phones (reading), 163–169
COVID-19 pandemic, impact, 93, 139–140
Cox, Courtney (menopause discussion), 52
Cushing's syndrome, 18–19, 179
Cyber-bullying, 95

D
Dating apps
   addiction, company goal, 152–155
   efficiency, 153
   problems, 151
Diagnostic and Statistical Manual of Mental Disorders (DSM-5), digital addiction, 95
Dietary Supplement Health and Education Act (DSHEA), 177
Diet, supplements (usage), 200–201
Diindolylmethane (DIM) (Superceutical ingredient), 183
Divorce (occurrence), smartphones (impact), 151
Dopamine, impact, 6, 153
Dorfman, Todd, 12, 34–35, 50, 54–57
   anxiety, 77
   hormone levels, news, 65
   HRT therapy, discussion, 70–71
   male symptoms, 68
   patients, physical reaction reporting, 86
   stress perspective, 79
   supplement goal, 186–187, 190
   vaginal dryness comments, 61

E
Efficiency mindset, negative impact, 140–141
Electromagnetic fields (EMFs), impact, 204–205
Emotional health, touch (impact), 162–163
Endings, loss, 12–14

Estrogen (sex hormone), 6
  fluctuations, severity
    (reduction), 66–67
  impact, 65
  reduction, 58–59, 63–64
Exercise
  negative impact, 201
  optimization, morning time
    (impact), 201–203
  workout intensity, reduction
    (decision), 202

F
Face-to-face interactions,
  positive impact, 136–138
Fat distribution, estrogen
  (impact), 64
Fear of Missing Out (FOMO)
  changes, 192–195
  impact, 191
  replacement, JOMO (usage),
    195–197
Focus, improvement, 205–206
Follow-up questions, asking,
  149–150
Food consumption
  content determination,
    199
  reduction, 197–200
Friendships
  interference, efficiency mindset
    (impact), 140–141

online connection, negative
  impact, 131
real-life friends,
  contact (importance),
    159–161

G
Gastroesophageal reflux disease
  (GERD), 56
Gathering spaces (erasure),
  technology (negative
  impact), 132–136
Ghosting, 155–156
Gracom, Alison, 7–9, 19, 29, 80,
  126, 159
Gratitude journaling, 208
Growth hormone, making
  (cessation), 19
Gummies
  ingredients (destruction),
    digestive system
    (impact), 187–188
  usage, problems/limitations,
    175–176

H
Habits, impact, 211
Heartburn, cortisol (impact),
  16–17
Heart, stress (impact),
  86–87
Hopf, Pat, 37–38

Hormone replacement therapy
(HRT)
  benefit, 70–71
  discontinuation, 71
  issues, 66–69
  study, 54
Hormones
  blue light, impact, 98–100
  body production, 25, 34–35
  chemical function, 6
  replenishment, sleep
    requirement, 26–28
Hot flashes, 51–53, 62
  system, rebalancing, 53–54
Hugs (fear), COVID social
  distancing (impact),
  161–163
Human growth hormone
  (HGH), secretion,
  32, 34
  stimulation, 185
Hypogonadism, 70

I
In-person connections,
  importance, 144–147
In-person interactions, 137–138
In real life (IRL) time, change, 94
Insomnia, estrogen/progesterone
  (impact), 63
Institutional review board (IRB)
  open label study, 54, 179

Intimacy
  deepening, 215
  relationship indicator, 169

J
Joy of Missing Out (JOMO)
  benefit, 197
  usage, 191, 195–197

L
Lawson, Jo, 96
Life
  balance, absence, 7
  reclaiming, 218–220
Losses, stress, 4
L-Theanine (Superceutical
  ingredient), 183
L-Tryptophan (Superceutical
  ingredient), 183–184

M
Maca (Superceutical ingredient),
  184
Magnolia bark
  (Superceutical
  ingredient), 184–185
Mattress, impact, 37–39
Media. *See* Social media
  multitasking, 121, 205
Medicine, gender bias, 50
Melatonin (Superceutical
  ingredient), 185

Melatonin secretion, 41
  reliance, 31
  suppression, body (impact), 40
Menopause
  body/emotional fluctuations, 51–53
  cortisol, role, 73
  discussion/ads, 48
  doctors, assistance (problem), 49–51
  grace, allowance, 74
  impact, 60–65
  relief, cortisol (impact), 47
  solutions, 66
  symptoms, 68–69
    management, 56
    reduction, 179–180
  treatment, HRT (usage), 67–69
  understanding/treatment options, 56–57
  unpredictability, 62–63
  women bodies, changes, 57–60
Mental health
  social media, connection, 115–116
  touch, impact, 162–163
Metabolism
  cortisol, impact, 7–8
  jumpstarting, 201
Mindfulness techniques, usage, 208

Modern love, current behaviors, 164–165
Mood swings, reasons, 65
Motivation (death), multitasking (impact), 120–121

N

National Sleep Foundation Sleep in America (poll), 37
Networks, creation (problem), 145
Night sweats, 62–63
Nighttime routine, initiation, 216
Non-Rapid Eye Movement (NREM), 32

O

Oat straw (Superceutical ingredient), 185–186
Online connection, negative impact, 131
Online dating
  addiction, company goal, 152–155
  anonymity, behaviors, 155–156
  dark side, 154
  habits, development (problems), 156–158
  limitations, 151
Online friends, reality/illusion, 145
Oxytocin, impact, 6

P

Pancreas, insulin pumping (continuation), 15–16
Parenting, troubles, 212
Perimenopause, 57
Phubbing, impact, 165
Physical touch, impact, 159–161
Pills
 ingredients (destruction), digestive system (impact), 187–188
 usage, problems/limitations, 175–176
Progesterone (sex hormone), 6
 fluctuations, severity (reduction), 66–67
 reduction, 58–59, 63–64
Push notifications
 cell phone use, correlation, 104–105
 impact, 101–108

R

Rapid Eye Movement (REM), 32, 35
Real dating (replacement), online dating (impact), 158
Real-life connection
 continuation, importance, 170–171
 social media, negative impact, 144–147
Real-life dating, return (reasons), 170
Real-life encounters, technology replacement (losses), 141–144
Real-life freedom, 211
Real-life friends, contact (importance), 159–161
Real-life social skills/community, reclaiming (steps), 147–150
Rebalance Health
 benefits, 45
 cortisol management, 72–73
 creation, reasons, 21–22
 studies, results, 180
 testing, 53–54
Rebalance Health System, change maker, 189–190
Rebalance Hot Flash System, IRB approval, 179
Rebalance products (clinical testing results), reliance (reasons), 178–180
Rebalance Superceuticals®
 balance, naming (reasons), 180–187
 Lozenges, usage, 175
Red light, impact, 41–42
Reishi mushroom (Superceutical ingredient), 186

Relationship
  destruction, FOMO (usage), 191
  healing, food (impact), 197–200
  improvement, phones (nonusage), 206–207
  intimacy, relationship satisfaction (increase), 167
  satisfaction
    increase, 167
    phubbing, impact, 165
  success (failure), online dating habits (impact), 156–158

S
Schultz, Howard, 132
Screens
  school battles, 122–123
  time
    excess, negative impact, 119–120
    reduction, 203–205, 215
  Screen Time Tracker data, 109–110
Seasonal Affective Disorder (SAD), 39
Self-esteem, harm, 198
Serotonin, impact, 184
Sex hormones, production, 5
Sex life, menopause (impact), 60–62

Silicon Valley companies, intrusion, 203–204
Skills (erasure), online connection (impact), 131
Sleep
  aids, problems, 45–46
  bedtime, practices, 124–127
  broken sleep (avoidance), JOMO (usage), 191
  cycle, disturbance, 63
  deprivation, problems, 25–27
  disruption
    blue light, impact, 40, 98–101
    red light, impact, 41–42
  hygiene, 46f
  importance, 25
  improvement, advice, 36–37
  loss, 30, 81–82
    smart phone screens, impact, 39–40, 42–44
  menopause, impact, 63–64
  priority, 123–124
  revolution, mattress (impact), 37–39
  schedule, requirement, 30–32, 33
  timing, 28–30
  trouble, 35
  types, 32–33
  understanding, 28

Sleep Number Bed, impact, 37–39
Sleep-wake cycle, hormone control, 40
Slow-wave sleep (SWS) (deep sleep), 32
Smartphones
- addictiveness/addiction, 91–92, 204
- entrepreneur/company profits, 91, 104–108
- computer capabilities, 92–94
- contents, impact, 96–97
- exclusion, feelings, 165
- harm, 91
- negative impact, 96–98, 136–137
- screens
  - impact, 39–40, 42–44
  - limitation, 205–206
- time, reclaiming (benefit), 207–209
- usage, management, 109–111
Social decorum (changes), COVID (impact), 162
Social distancing
- effects, recovery, 139–140
- hugs, fear, 161–163
Social interaction (problems), technology (impact), 143–144

Social media
- attachment, problematic type, 193
- danger, 116–117
- negative impact, 115–116, 144–147
Social skills (disappearance), technology (impact), 82–83
Starbucks (gathering spaces erasure), technology (negative impact), 132–136
Steroid hormone, 8
Strategies, impact, 211
Stress
- anxiety, contrast, 76–78
- cortisol, impact, 79
- cycle, rhythm problems, 125
- elimination, understanding, 217
- experience, 3–4
- impact, 75
- increase, 199–200
- meaning, 10–11
- normality, 78–79
- push notifications, impact, 101–108
- response, 4–5
- understanding, 79–82
Stress-free life, 16

Supplements
  goal, 186–187
  impacts, 211
  labels, misleading aspect, 177–178
  manufacturer studies, absence/nonrequirement, 176–177
Synaptic pruning, long-term effects, 31

T
Takotsubo cardiomyopathy (TCM) (broken heart syndrome), 86–87
Technology
  addiction
    problem, 22–23
    WHO identification, 95
  addictive nature, JOMO rejection, 195
  benefits/dangers, 94–95
  negative impact, 83–84, 132–136
  progression, 97
  revolution, safeguards (absence), 108–109
Teenagers (targeting), adult predators (impact), 117–118

Testosterone (sex hormone), 6
  fluctuations, severity (reduction), 66–67
  reduction, 55, 58–59, 63–64
  replacement, risk, 71–72
Third-party apps, impact, 106–107
Thyroid hormones, menopause (impact), 64
Time
  loss, 213
  reclaiming, benefit, 207–209

U
UK Million Women Study, 67
Unstructured play, AI (children usage), 130
Urgency (false sense, creation), technology/FOMO (impact), 196

V
Vaginal dryness, menopause symptom, 61

W
Wakefulness (2 A.M.), reason, 35–36
Walker, Bob, 37–38

Watts, Naomie (menopause discussion), 52
Weight gain, menopause (impact), 64–65
Wellbeing, harm, 198
Well-being (foundation), healthy habits (usage), 200–201
Well-being, path, 87–88
Women (bodies change), menopause (impact), 57–60
Women's Health Initiative (WHI) trial, 67